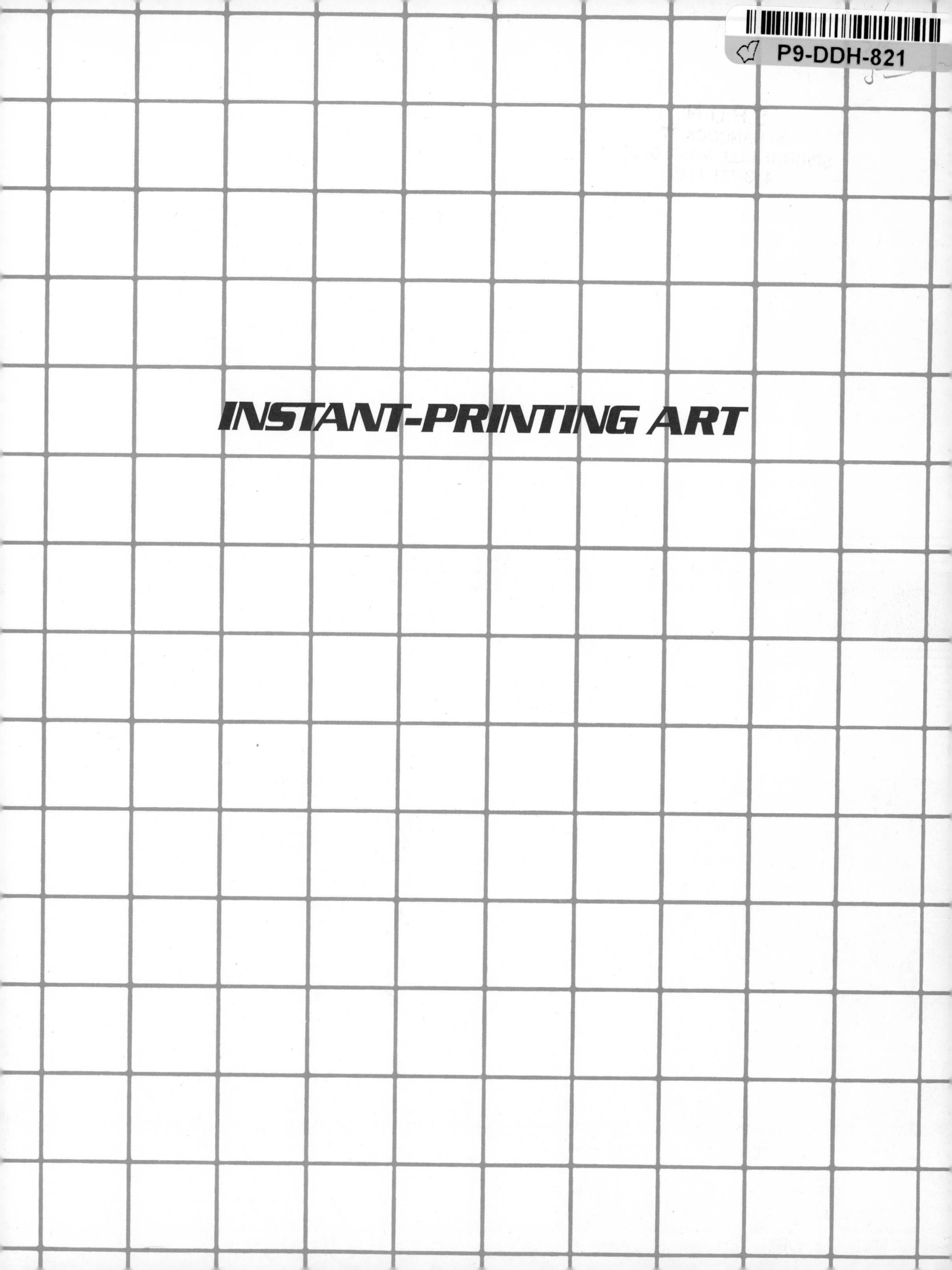
INSTANT-PRINTING ART

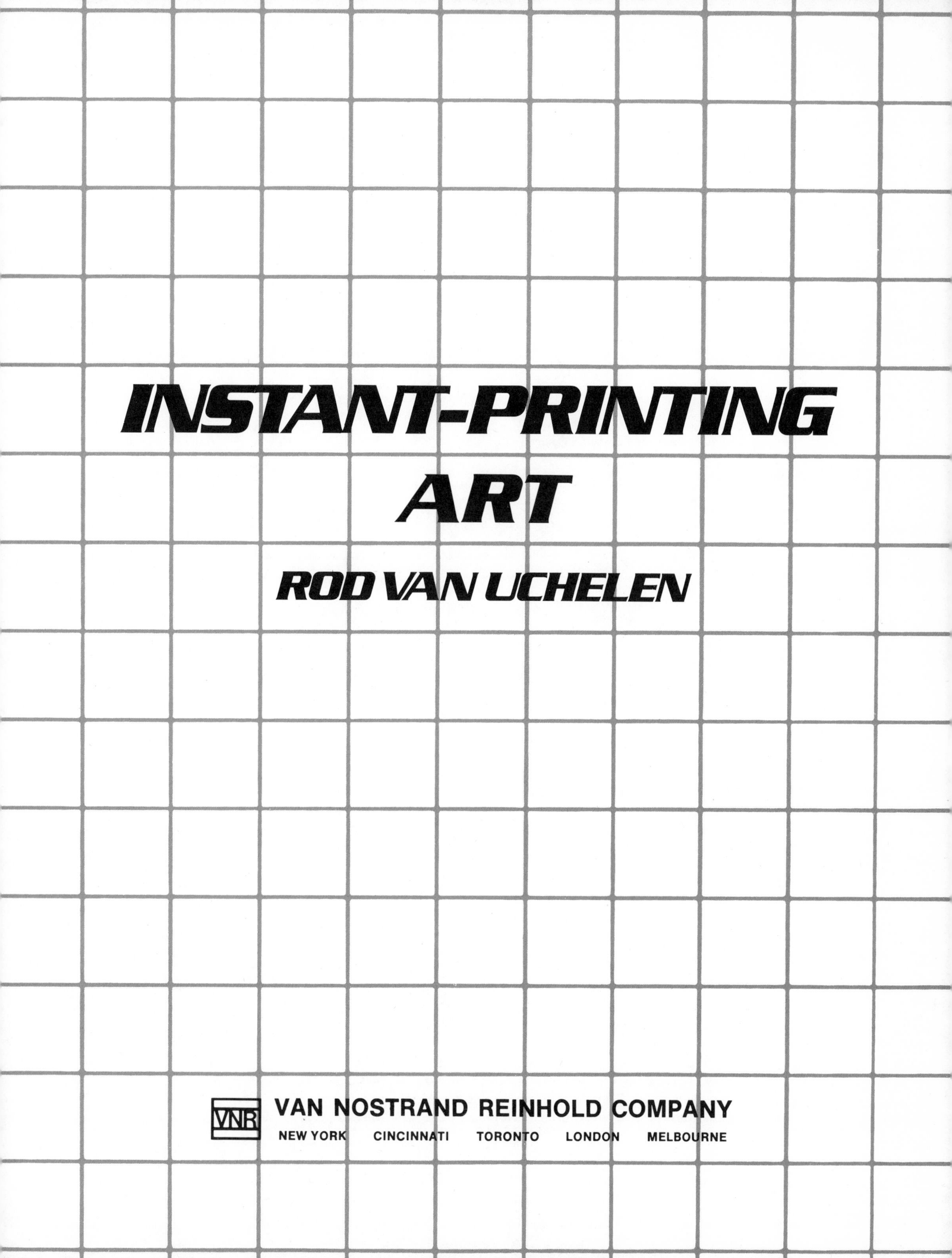

INSTANT-PRINTING ART

ROD VAN UCHELEN

VNR VAN NOSTRAND REINHOLD COMPANY
NEW YORK CINCINNATI TORONTO LONDON MELBOURNE

Library of Congress Catalog Card Number 82-17365
ISBN 0-442-29037-3

Printed in the United States of America
Designed by Patricia H. Ten

Published by Van Nostrand Reinhold Company Inc.
135 West 50th Street
New York, New York 10020

Fleet Publishers
1410 Birchmount Road
Scarborough, Ontario M1P 2E7, Canada

Van Nostrand Reinhold
480 Latrobe Street
Melbourne, Victoria 3000, Australia

Van Nostrand Reinhold Company Limited
Molly Millars Lane
Wokingham, Berkshire RG11 2PY, England

16 15 14 13 12 11 10 9 8 7 6 5 4 3 2 1

Library of Congress Cataloging in Publication Data

van Uchelen, Rod.
Instant-printing art.

Includes index.
1. Printing, Instant. I. Title.
Z252.5.I49V36 1983 686.2′254 82-17365
ISBN 0-442-29037-3

Acknowledgments

A number of people have generously contributed their art and designs to this book. Thanks are due to Mrs. Lamonta Pierson, Mr. Arnold Carlson, Ms. Barbara Kelly, Mr. Gonzalo Duran, Mr. Bill Dalziel, and David Ziller. Special thanks are due to the Bloom franchise of PIP, and also to Chan Printing.

CONTENTS

INTRODUCTION

In the past the printer provided whatever materials were necessary for printing; the buyer had only to tell the printer what was wanted and that took care of everything. With offset lithography and instant printing this is no longer true, and the printer does not supply the material for printing, but only prints the image provided by the customer.

Since the instant printer does not supply typesetting, art, or design as part of the printing service, the customers can design their own product with these materials. The "instant" part of instant printing is that one no longer has to wait for material to be made up by the printer.

The process used for instant printing was originally intended as a reprographic process for the duplication of business material, primarily that produced on a typewriter. The process originated as a result of improvements in photographic materials when these are used to make a printing plate. When more than a few copies are needed, the process is cheaper, quicker, and better than copiers or comparable methods.

The process applied to instant printing is so satisfactory and so convenient in fact, that it has become an ubiquitous industry with shops in most high-traffic areas. It is utilized not only for reprography but also for general low-quantity printing. If small quantities of a product are needed, then instant printing is the most economic process: for a few dollars several hundred copies can be produced. The uses of instant printing are continually expanding simply because it is so inexpensive.

The quality of instant printing is suitable for many different kinds of products. If it is not comparable to the traditional methods of job printing, the difference in cost makes it the chosen technique, particularly when additional services are available from the same supplier.

What is instant printing? What does it produce and how does one use it? Answering these questions is the purpose of this book. You can do it your way.

MAJOR PRINCIPLES 1

Printing is always thought of as a manufacturing industry, but in the case of instant or quick printing it is more appropriate to think of it as a service industry. It is the service aspect, the speed, that constitutes the quick part of instant printing—focusing on duplication instead of fabrication. It may be viewed as a service. Just as an originator must supply a secretary with information to be typed, a user of instant printing must present the printer with material to be duplicated. The process simply repeats what the user provides; the user is the fabricator.

This differentiation between manufacturing and service is important for a number of reasons. One of the more significant consequences is that the instant printer is spared the proofing process because he is not involved in the fabrication. The typesetting, assembly, and the checking of the materials is entirely the responsibility of the originator. The job of the instant printer is solely to reproduce the original with photographic accuracy, and this is what permits the instant response and makes a retail activity of the printing process.

There were technical developments that made retail selling of printing possible. These were the result of improvements in photographic materials, the techniques that permit the direct exposure of the printing plate, and the development of low-cost paper plates for offset printing. But these developments, while greatly simplifying and speeding the process, did not alone produce the industry of instant printing; any lithography printer could use them. It was the change in marketing in tandem with these techniques that made it possible.

1-1, 1-2. Instant printing provides a simplification of the steps needed to prepare the art and do printing. The first four steps prepare the art, and the next four produce the printing.

And the concept of combining a new technology with service produces something distinctively new to the graphic industry.

Behind the concept of instant printing is a great deal of restructuring of the printing process, all of it based on quick turnaround time and retail selling. As a result of these new developments, the instant printer's services are expanding. He now often supplies a copying service for small-quantity duplication on a copier. Additional services offered are trimming, folding, collating, drilling, stapling, binding, padding, stuffing, and others, some more related to office services than to printing.

The terminology for instant printing services is that of traditional printing, even though the basis for their performance is different. These services have now been simplified to function with direct image technology, facilitating retail selling and speed.

Instant printing is not a craft-oriented business, as is traditional printing, but service-oriented. It has a relationship to craft in that its services take their format from those of custom printing. This provides for mass production with options, so that the use of a colored ink, for example, is possible for an extra

WHAT WE CAN DO ON OUR XEROX MACHINES

- REDUCTION
- ENLARGEMENT
- ADDRESS LABELS
- TRANSPARENCIES
- 2 SIDED COPIES
- OVERSIZE COPIES
- COLOR COPIES
- PRINT ON YOUR PAPER
- AND VARIOUS STOCK

1-3. The copier is also used for duplication, but for fewer copies than are possible with instant printing. There are large electrostatic copiers with an imaging system that produces a copy with only small differences in quality from that of instant printing. In addition these copiers can be used to prepare art for instant printing.

charge. Even within the framework of mass production, however, the element of craft is necessarily inherent in instant printing, because all the processes are under the operator's control. Skill is a considerable factor in the resulting product.

This kind of printing is essentially designed to provide the user with a printer's services at the retail level. The simplification that characterizes the process imposes a number of restrictions on the user, who in order to deal with them needs to understand them. The essential principles are this simplification, the format used to achieve it, the mechanical requirements of the direct-image process, and the requirements for preparing material for the different printing services.

SIMPLIFICATION

One way to deal with simplification is to start with the basic unit. For instant printing that unit might be said to be a standard 8½ × 11 inch notepaper-sized sheet. This serves as a module for the others and a premise for considering the systematic organization of instant printing. This systematization is in contrast with regular printing, where the premise is a custom approach, where the printer handles a variety of requirements. The focus is on the product, not the process.

Instant printing, however, requires that the product fit a structured process. Standardization is the means of simplification. When planning a product, the user should think of the category into which the item will fit. The innovative concept behind instant printing is the restructuring. The sheet as a unit is contrary to the regular printing custom of placing the image on an oversized sheet and then trimming it to the product size. In instant printing the standard sheet size offered by the printer is often the product size. By not having to carry an infinite array of paper sizes the printer can maintain a standardized inventory of standard measures. Paper types and qualities are many and varied. The instant printer, however, stocks only a

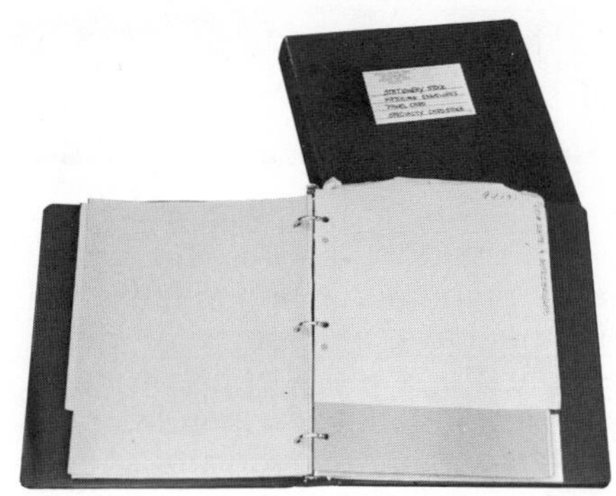

1-5. Samples of the papers stocked are shown in a notebook, and the user makes the selection.

few grades well suited to the process.

This kind of simplification makes the printer comparable to a retailer with an inventory and provides for quick service. The customary practice is to use the paper manufacturer or wholesaler for inventory, ordering a particular paper for each job. The simplification extends to printing plate materials, inks, photo equipment, printing presses and press sizes, and equipment to handle subsequent operations.

An instant printer's equipment is designed and set up with permanent jigs to handle standard sizes; the printing custom is to make the set up for each job. This allows the instant printer to simplify. As an example of how this works, the printer inks the press with a black ink suitable for the grades of paper he is selling, and the press is ready when the jobs come in. Because the sizes fit the standard set up, they can be done immediately. The usual printing practice, on the other hand, is to design the ink for the paper to be used and the color for the job and finally to put both ink and paper on the press. With the completion of the run the press is washed. The instant printer does not wash the press until the close of the day after a series of jobs. The instant printer

1-4. A large variety of products can be printed with instant printing formats, as this display of attractive, well-designed products shows.

in effect handles a series of jobs as one job. Fewer kinds of printing jobs are offered and many of these are done immediately.

Traditional job printing with its complexities and variations gained printers an unenviable reputation for never having their work done when expected. A printing press runs fast, and the mechanical process of duplication is not nearly so unpredictable as the problems that occur when ordering materials and fabricating set ups for one-of-a-kind products.

When the designing and assembling of the material to be printed is handled by the user and not the printer, the worst difficulties are cleared away, and the printer's work is enormously eased.

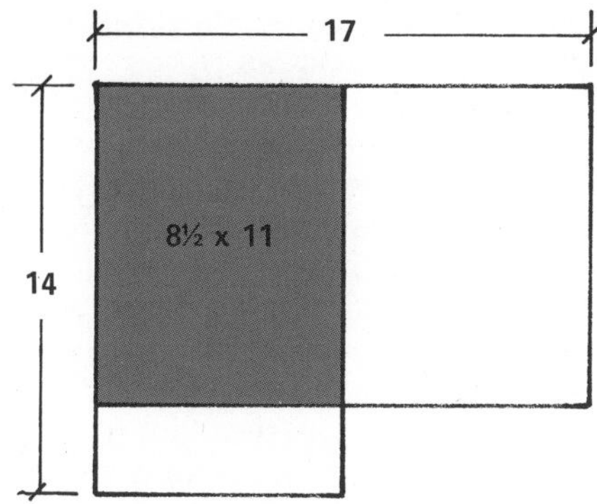

1-6. Seeing the relationship between the three format sizes of paper stock is a help in remembering them. Two sizes may be thought of as variants of the basic 8½ × 11 inch size.

Offset lithography printing needs only the image for reproduction, and it is copied photographically. Another simplification. No longer is it necessary to assemble each piece of material with raised portions designed to take the ink and make the image. Whatever strongly contrasted image is presented to the printing plate can be reproduced as printing. Only the image is required, so it is possible for the user to prepare the material for duplication.

In traditional offset printing the fabrication of material has normally been handled by various professionals: designers, artists, typesetters, and photographers. But instant printing, however, is related to reprography, in which material is produced at the level of office quality. This does not exclude the use of various professional services in preparing material, though. An example might be the substitution of professional typesetting for the typewriter.

Since it is possible to put anything graphic on an 8½ × 11 inch sheet, the user has almost unlimited scope. It is possible to produce any number of products within the simplified instant-printing format. All that is needed is to relate the product to the format requirements.

FORMAT

The restructuring that instant printing imposes on the printing process can be described as a format that products must accommodate to. The 8½ × 11 inch size sheet may be called the basic module; though arbitrary, this is a starting point. Standard paper sizes extend from the basic unit to a double size of 17 × 11 inches. In addition there is the standard legal size sheet of 8½ × 14 inches. These three sizes, all related to the 8½ × 11 inch size, are almost universally agreed upon as the standard formats. Exceptions might include standard sizes such as quarto. Instant-printing franchises are now expanding to Europe.

It is important to remember that the small presses used are built to take a maximum size of 17 × 11 inches and that the photosensitized printing plates are made in the three sizes that correspond to the standard paper sizes. When the material to be duplicated does not conform exactly to these standard dimensions, most printers can adjust the size of the material photographically as it is copied onto the printing plate.

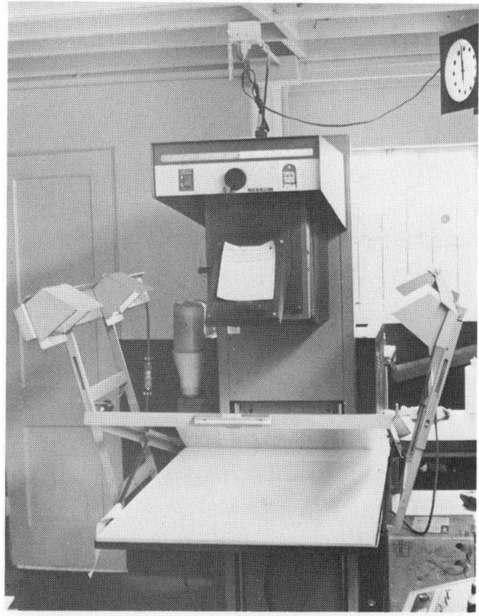

1-7, 1-8. An instant-printing camera looks like a graphic arts camera. Instead of making film negatives, it makes the printing plate directly. The scale at the top of the camera is used to adjustments when making size changes in the art.

Some of the more popular equipment permits enlarging the material to 110 percent of its original size or reducing it to as little as 50 percent of its original size. Thus the resulting printed piece can be larger or smaller than the original, though most printers make an extra charge for this adjustment.

The size of paper that the original material is on is not the concern. Rather it is the size of the image on the original material and its relation to the format paper sizes. Thus it is conceivable that material floating on an 8½ × 14 sheet could be properly centered on an 8½ × 11 inch sheet without any size change.

Pricing is based on the 8½ × 11 inch printed sheet and the quantity. The prices are given for the standard bond paper in stock, printed on one or two sides. Usually, in stock are another better grade of bond paper with rag content and often specialty papers. Larger sizes and quantity increase the price, as do specialty papers. The latter may be those with a special surface, such as a leather finish, or those in heavier weight, like card stock. The instant printer may also stock gum-backed or adhesive-backed papers. All these are stocked in white.

Because the press is set up with black ink, most instant printers gain an effect of color by stocking colored papers and card stock. On hand are yellow, blue, pink, green, buff, and often additional shades of each color. Specialty papers may be stocked only in white.

Also in stock are envelopes in the standard number 10 business size in white and in all the colors carried. Often there is enough call for the number 9 envelope that fits inside the number 10 to warrant carrying it. Perhaps they also stock window envelopes. In addition square baronial envelopes may also be carried in a few sizes that are multiples of a folded 8½ × 11 inch sheet.

With the press set up and inked, any of these papers may be taken off the shelf and printed. The time it takes for the printing plate to be exposed, developed, and positioned on the press is the time it takes to make ready for printing. The plate, make-ready, and press run are handled in a matter of minutes for a particular job. Even a short queue does not cause a long wait, when there are people to handle the customers. The press may go from job to job with only a change of plate, its positioning, and a quick cleaning of the plate and blanket to clear and re-ink it for the next run.

1-9. Small offset presses produce instant printing from a one-step plate. Using a format of paper sizes, they run from job to job with a minimum of makeready.

This is how the format works and why prices can be so low for small quantities. Work outside the format is held until it is changed for the new specifications. Envelope jobs, for example, are run one after another at the end of the day, using the same set up. Work requiring special services is also done in off-hours. If material is to be trimmed, time is needed for the ink to dry before the sheets are squeezed together, while being held in the trimmer.

Depending on the size of the shop and the number of presses, printers vary in the sizes immediately available for work. Many prefer to operate a number of presses in the 8½ × 11 format, since the majority of their work is done in this size. Other format sizes are offered as a one-day service, when such jobs can be grouped. Plates for other sizes are made as quickly by the same direct process and handled in the same manner. Direct image printing plates, produced in less than a minute, are the low-cost items that make possible the inexpensive printing of small quantity jobs.

DIRECT IMAGE

Instant printing uses a small offset lithography press. Lithography utilizes only the image for printing, and offset lithography simply means that the image is offset from the printing plate to a printing blanket and thence to the paper. This allows the original image on the printing plate to be right reading. That is, the material reads from left to right as is normal, instead of reading the wrong way, as in a mirror image. It appears exactly as the printed piece will look.

The image on the printing plate is made directly from the art. There are no steps between the art and exposing the plate to the art. This is why the printing plate is called a direct-image plate. This process goes from from the positive image on the art to the positive image on the printing plate, reversing the mode of the photosensitized surface. Normally photography moves from the positive to the negative and back to the positive, as in traditional printing. Conventional offset lithography uses film negatives to make the printing plate. With the art exposed onto negatives, the negatives are assembled and used to expose the printing plate, rather like using a film negative to print a photograph.

With the direct image plate there is no manipulation of the art in the printing process, and the art should be presented exactly as it is wanted in the reproduction. It is only when negatives are used between the art and the printing plate that there is an opportunity to adjust the image before it is exposed. The direct image plate by removing these in-between steps simplifies the process and lowers the cost. The use of different materials, as opposed to the conventional ones, also economizes. Direct image plates are called paper plates be-

1-10. Another camera, it works on an electrostatic principle to produce printing plates. The importance to the user is that it is panchromatic, not orthochromatic, and registers all colors instead of only the ones at the red end of the spectrum. This means that if blue construction lines are dark they will register on the printing plate, and worse, they cannot be removed easily from the printing plate. 3M® also markets the same kind of platemaker, which is orthochromatic. The switches in the foreground control the density of exposure, so that the plate reproduces what is wanted from the copy.

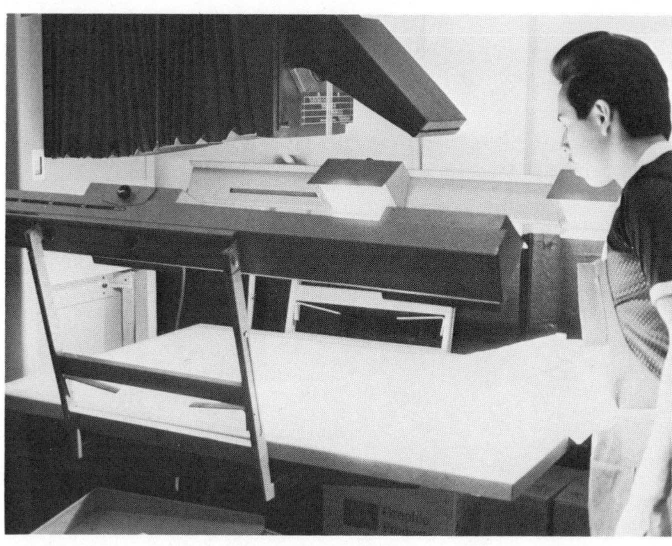

1-11. The graphic camera needs a brilliant light to make the exposure. The operator is "dodging" during exposure, holding back portions of the art from printing by blocking the reflected light.

cause the photosensitizing is mounted on what looks like paper but is actually a plastic composition with wet strength. The sensitized base for a conventional printing plate is an aluminum sheet.

The exposure is due to the reflectance of the art and copy, with the film responding to the reflected light. Therefore, differences in the reflectance of the art will change the relative exposure. A glossy surface that reflects more light than a matte surface will expose more quickly. The best results are always obtained by using art and copy that have a uniformly dense black image on a bright, white, matte surface of even reflectance. The emulsion does compensate, though, for a degree of discrepancy.

The sensitized plate uses a high-contrast ortho-emulsion, and is designed to react by either exposing or not developing. There are no in-between positions of partial printing; the plate must resolve into print or no-print. Orthochromatic emulsion is not equally sensitive to all colors. It responds to red most strongly and to blue the most weakly, with the other colors falling in between. Since colors also have a black and white value, it takes a fine judgment to decide whether colored art and copy can be held for duplication, or not. If the color to be copied is red, there is usually no problem, because the film sees red as if it were black. At the other extreme, a pale blue will be invisible to the orthochromatic emulsion. Black lettering against a pale blue field might be copied by dropping out the blue. The same black letters against a red field could not be copied because the red would expose at the same value as the black.

Manipulation of the art on a direct image plate must be limited to blocking and dodging during exposure. When blocking, certain portions of the art are covered with blank pieces of paper, and dodging is the holding back of certain areas of the art to gain a more balanced exposure. An object is moved between these areas and the lens.

Colors do not expose at the same value as clear black and white, but depending on the configuration of the art, blocking and dodging can be used in some degree to compensate. There is usually an extra charge for dealing with this kind of problem. Sometimes it is simplest to get a color-corrected print, in which the color is balanced with filters.

Type

BLACK & WHITE

BLACK & COLOR

COLOR & WHITE

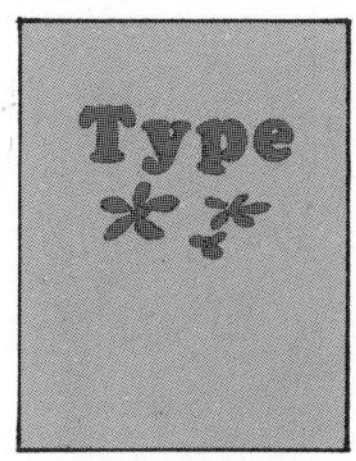

COLOR & COLOR

1-12. Color on the art makes a difference in the exposure because of the density of the image. Conventional graphic arts film is orthochromatic, which allows use of pale blue construction lines, because they are invisible to the film.

1-13. The printing plate can be cleaned up a little. Here a hard eraser is used to remove a blemish produced by the art, so that it will not reproduce on the printed material.

The final step that can be taken to correct the printing plate is to remove blemishes and marks made by shadows at the edges of pieces of paper or by dirt on the art outside the image. If not too pronounced, these are removed by scraping away the emulsion. This must be handled carefully so as not to disturb the image or the surface of the plate. The direct image plate is capable of a nice fidelity to the copy, when it is presented correctly. Problems often arise when color is presented to a system not designed to handle it.

Though some adjustments can be made in the exposure of the plate and minor blemishes removed, it is plain that this kind of plate is designed for speed and economy and is integrated into a system meant to provide quick service. It is not designed for custom work. When that is needed, it is better done as artwork. This uses the system to its best advantage and provides for the highest quality of printing from the direct image plate.

SERVICES

Services offered by instant printers are primarily used after printing. In a sense they are similar to those of a conventional bindery and involve the further development of printed matter into product form. They are usually enumerated and priced by the unit, so the user can elect to use them as preferred.

Each is a printing term. They are:

Collating—gathering the printed sheets into a particular order. It is priced by the hundred sheets and has a minimum charge.

Drilling—making holes in the printed piece for use with a ring binder. It is priced by the hole per hundred sheets and has a minimum charge.

Padding—gluing the edge of printed sheets to form a pad. It is priced by the pad with a minimum.

Folding—machine folding of the printed piece. It is priced by the fold per hundred sheets with a minimum.

Stapling—binding a group of printed sheets. It is priced by the staple with a minimum.

Cutting—trimming the printed sheet to product size. It is priced by the cut with a minimum.

None of these is a while-you-wait service, because the printed sheets must be dry before they can be worked on. Dealing with small quantities, these processes can be done by hand. As the quantity increases, it may be advisable to pay the service charge for machine work. The decision is usually made on a time-against-cost basis and depends to some extent on the type of product wanted.

Though instant printing is in no way connected with designing and assembling the product, many instant printers have found it useful to offer a simple mechan-

1-14. These basic services done after printing make it possible to extend the variety of products that can be made with instant printing.

ical paste-up service to assemble multiples. Such a service has extra charges for the copies and for the paste-up of these copies into multiples. The user can easily perform these steps by having the printing done in two stages: one, to provide the multiples, two, to provide the quantity. A decision is again made on a cost-against-time basis.

The decision to print in multiples usually follows the line of least cost. Since anything that can be run in multiples must be smaller than the sheet size, the charges include the cutting service. One compares the quantity-needed charge plus the cutting cost against the multiple-run charge plus preparation and cutting cost.

In arbitrary figures suppose that the cost of printing a thousand is $26 plus $2 for trimming. This gives a total of $28. By running five up—a multiple of five—the quantity could be two hundred, because 200 × 5 gives the needed quantity of a thousand. The cost of printing two hundred is $10. Preparation cost is $3 for the copies plus $3 for the paste-up for a total of $6. The additional trimming brings the cutting charge to $3. The total of service charges is $10 plus $6 plus $3 or $19. Now the $19 cost of the multiple run is compared to the $28 cost of the single run. In this example the multiple run saves $9.

Obviously the difference between the two printing prices must exceed the preparation cost to run multiples. When preparation is handled by the user, the multiple run is always least cost. The instant printer who offers these services will advise the user as to the best choice.

For the user it is helpful to understand the operations, because then the most economical course may be planned. If the problem isn't complicated, a phone call will do, but when the user visits, the instant printer can offer examples of what can be done with the system and the paper in stock.

The instant printer's machines are smaller than those for conventional, commercial printing. In all fairness it should be observed that with larger quantities the instant printer is not equipped to achieve the economies possible with the larger equipment of a conventional printer. Conversely the conventional printer cannot deal with services and small jobs at the price of the instant printer. Gathering and collating separate sheets, for example, is fine in small quantities, but with larger quantities a conventional job printer would achieve the same thing by folding signatures. When folded, these signatures have all the pages in the right order and will be trimmed to release them into separate pages.

The instant printer presents services in a unique way, when compared to conventional printing. Drilling applies to instant printing and its use is primarily for a ring binder. Folding can be done in a variety of ways, but the instant printer is most often set up to do only parallel folds, like the ones in a business letter. Padding has its obvious relationship to forms and note pads. Stapling is but one way of binding material permanently. Through these services, the instant printing format can be used to make all kinds of business and personal products inexpensively.

PRODUCTS 2

When we think of printing, we think of the end result. But the successful use of instant printing requires some understanding of the process, because the user must be intimately involved with it in selecting services and planning and preparing material. The awareness with which this is done has a direct effect on the results.

The following products have been selected because they have proved popular. They are examples not only of specific products but also of a number of variations that a little practice makes possible to the innovative user through the inexpensive services of this printing process.

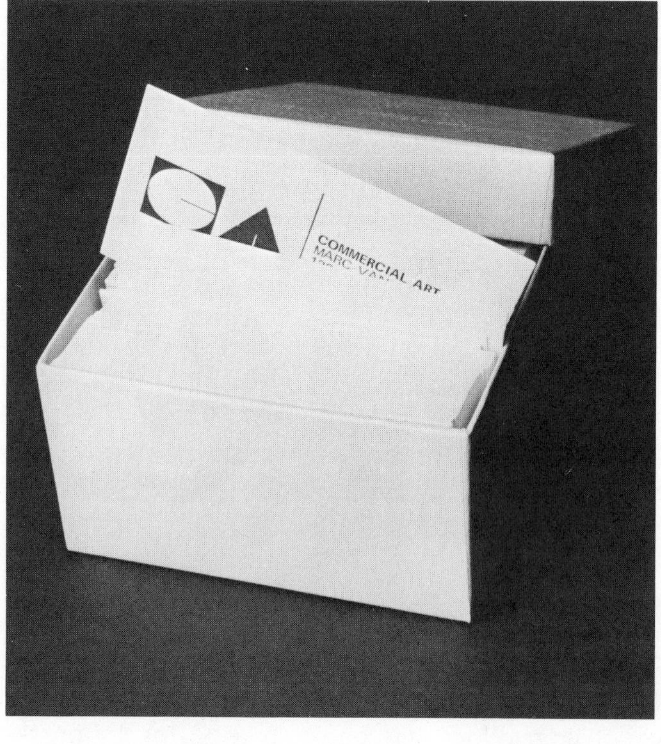

2-1. Business cards might head the list of printed products needed for a small business.

PRODUCTS FOR BUSINESS

These products, more often than not, are extremely useful to small businesses, which have the same need as big businesses for support from printed material. Since they differ only in not requiring large quantities, instant printing is made to order.

These commonly used products are not in any special order, though business cards might easily head the list.

The convenience of having business activity, name, address, and phone number all available on one bit of paper makes a business card a useful item. (Women working alone from their homes sometimes limit for security reasons the amount of information on their cards, adding the address and phone number when handing them out.)

Because of the usefulness of a business card as a form of advertising for business prospects, there may be a temptation to overload it with information. And this creates problems in design and communication by tending to force the type to become smaller and more crowded in order to squeeze all the information into the space. It is far more reasonable to make the type comfortably readable. This is what hap-

BUSINESS CARDS come in all styles, but there is a conventional type, which tends to vary more in design than in dimension. The 3½ × 2 inch size is the one most often used, and the number of stationery items for storing this size is an argument for not using a larger card. If the design differs greatly from the conventional, the standard measurement still tends to identify the item as a business card.

2-2. The business card is a standard size, but the simplification of the design is not conventional.

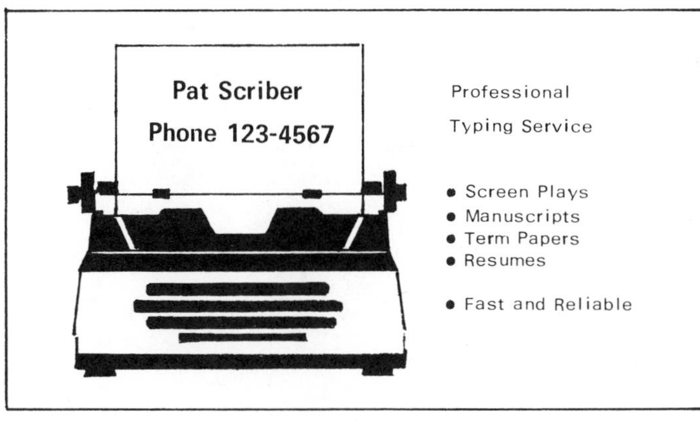

2-3. Squeezing too much information in tends to make the type too small. While the design is clear and understandable, slightly larger type would have improved readability.

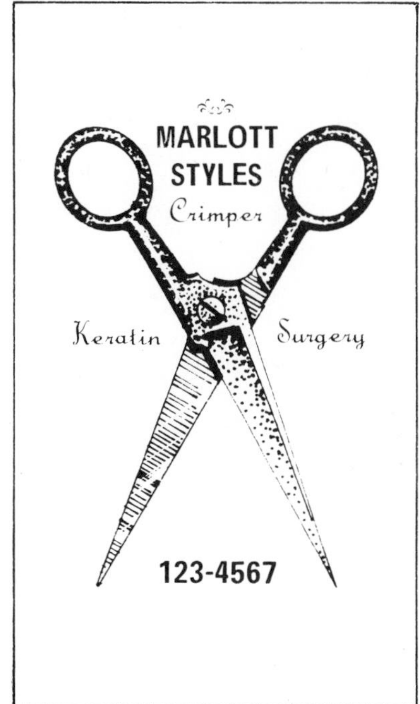

2-4. Barber's scissors are easily recognizable, yet this is an insider's design. Not many know that "crimper" is "Liverpoolese" for barber—except the customers in the music world to whom the card is directed. Keratin surgery, of course, is hair cutting, and the design that conveys the basic information makes a clever appeal to specific customers.

S & S interior refinishing

professional
paper hanging
interior painting

hans stucker
1234 hollywood blvd.
hollywood, ca 90000
(213) 123-4567

2-5. A business card design should get across the information simply and directly. Art adds to the appeal.

pens on those conventional cards that can be ordered in lots of a thousand and that are almost invariably printed in blue ink. The typesetter crams too much information into the standard locations, making them a good argument for less conventional design. With instant printing, on the other hand, the person who needs a card has the freedom to prepare a distinctively personal design and to order as few or as many as are needed.

The user's ingenuity is exercised in designing the card and in obtaining and preparing the material for printing. There is, of course, always the possibility of using an artist for this design and preparation, just as larger businesses do, but the cleverness of many non-professional designs provides incentive and inspiration. There are many ways to obtain material for the art. It is possible to reprint a business card, using the original card as the artwork. Some people use business checks or their phone book as ads. It is more appropriate, though, to order typesetting, because its sharpness and clarity contributes to the overall appearance of the design, which is then assembled and presented to the instant printer for duplication.

This printing process necessitates the copying of the completed design, so that more than one card can be printed on each sheet. The 3½ × 2 inch size permits fitting twelve copies on each 8½ × 11 inch sheet of index board. The copies for multiple printing can be made by the instant printer, as previously described. Depending on the card's design, copies might be made on a high-quality copier, such as the one known as the duplicator. Bet-

P.I.P. - THE GOOD PLACE

THIS PRINTING JOB
WAS DONE TO PERFECTION
BY - BRIAN FROBISHER

SPECIALIZING IN - A.B. DICK 360-369
NCR, ENVELOPES, 11X17, AND XEROX MAINT.

2-6. The conventional design may have an unconventional message. Looking closely at this design, you see in the seal a deterioration of the image, due to repeated copying—fourth generation.

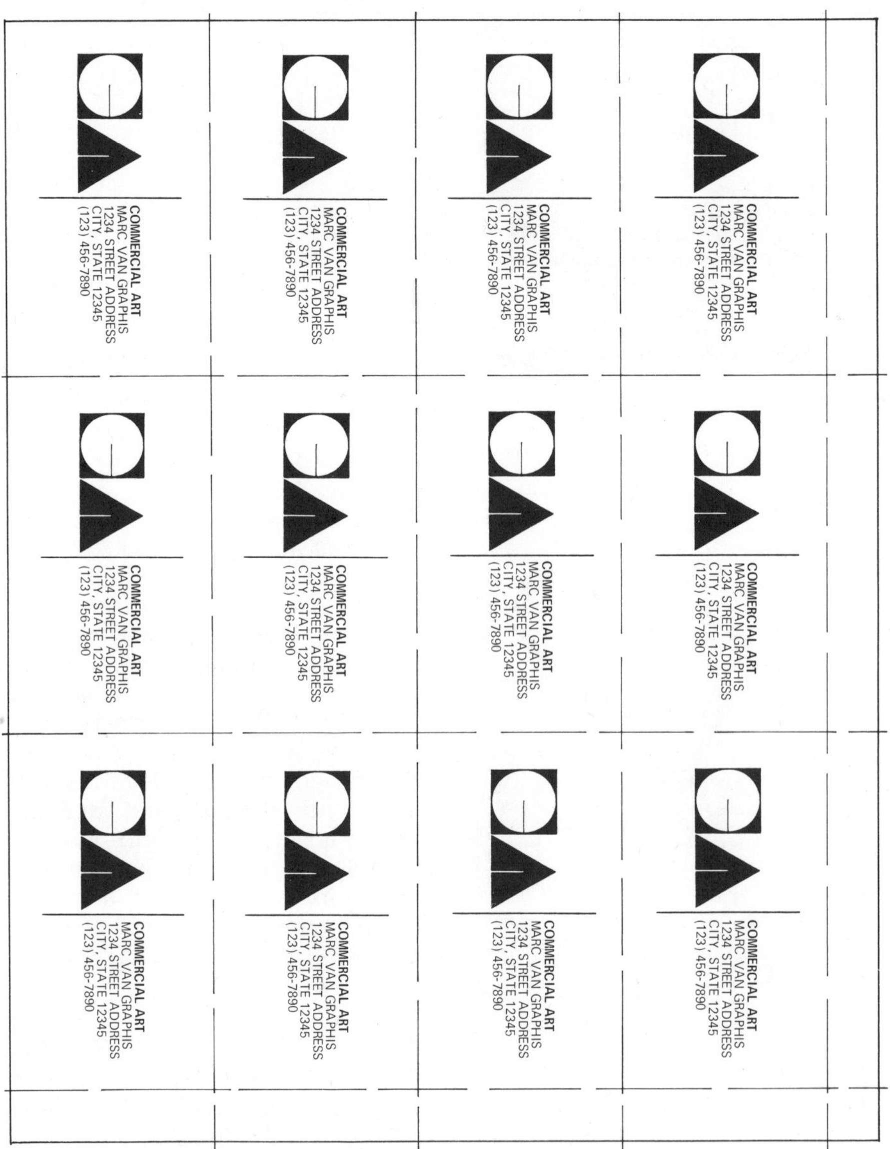

2-7. Copies of the card would be laid out this way for printing. The solid line represents the border of the sheet used for printing, and the broken line represents the trim.

ter yet, though more expensive, is using a photostat with a film image.

If a copier is used instead of instant printing to produce copies, it is essential that it be of the high resolution kind to preserve the type image and that it have the electrostatic process to hold the blackness. In general the instant-printing process will provide the better image, but the copier is suggested because it is so inexpensive.

The danger in copies is that the quality of the image deteriorates with subsequent ones, each being a step away from the original. At first, one might not notice a falling off of the image, but as a copy becomes a copy of a copy of a copy, the deterioration becomes quite noticeable. It is best to work as close to the original as possible and to use the finest process economically appropriate.

Copies of suitable quality are then arranged in three rows of four. They can be mounted so that they are clean and permanent, because they may be used again and again. It is worth noting that the copies used as art should be mounted in an exact square. The trimmer works to 90 degree angles, and if the art isn't on the sheet at the same angle, all the cuts will come out crooked when the sheet is trimmed into individual cards.

One way to minimize the risk of having the design seem uneven is to put nothing closer than ¼ inch from the edge. The closer to the edge the design gets, the more critical the trimming operation becomes and the more easily the eye sees even little variations in the finished product. For example, the kind of design that has a border around it will prove difficult, especially if the border is near the edges.

With twelve cards to the sheet, a small print order quickly becomes a large number of cards. Only fifty sheets will produce six hundred cards, and a hundred sheets produces 1,200 cards, and so on. On such a small print quantity, the cost for trimming will nearly equal the cost for printing. With a really small order, some might even find it advantageous to cut up their own sheets of cards, though hand trimming will never equal the uniformity and precision of the trimmer, which cuts cleanly through as many as five hundred at a time.

Remember that the low cost is predicated on using only black ink and standard stock. Two-color designs are tempting, but are they worth it? It involves putting a second color on the press, running the cards through again with the second color, and then washing-up the press. The cost for a second color will probably add as much again as the entire printing job in one color. The decision depends on one's budget for business cards.

If you do decide to add a second color to instant printing, be sure that the color position is not in a critical register, so that it must position to a line, for example. With instant printing, the press-feed will cause the position of the color to vary as much as 1/32 of an inch in some cases. The answer is not to have the color touch anything else or have a critical alignment. For example, if the CA logo on the accompanying illustration were to be in color, it might offer a problem because of the critical top and base alignment. Changing the design so that the type did not line up at top and bottom would remove the problem.

With the design of the logo and business card settled, it is much easier to proceed to the next logical item for a small business: stationery. The same logo is used for each and, in most cases, for the envelopes as well.

2-8. Stationery carries the logo design and the necessary information that was on the business card. The box size is a ream or five hundred sheets.

2-9. The stationery design is done in a straightforward way. The CA hangs over what will be the margin of the letter, and the information acts as a heading to the letter.

STATIONERY moves your business message. Like a business card, the mandatory information on a letter—name, address, and phone number—is an advertisement as well as a convenience.

For continuity, the same logo is generally used on all of a business' material. The design of the letterhead should take into account the form used in the presentation of a business letter. This form has placed the date and signature to the right of the margin for balance, but there is a growing use of the form that begins every line at the left-hand margin. The layout of the letterhead design may compensate for this by placing the logo to the right. A typical design has the logo to the left with the information to the right.

Since the art of business letter writing places great emphasis on brevity as well as clarity, the typical letter will not use all the page. This allows for further variety in placement and design. An additional variation places the letterhead information at the bottom with the logo alone at the top. Other designs use all four corners, top, bottom, or sides for logo information. Some of the wilder designs display art and pictures, and some have a cartouche or border around the area where the letter will be typed.

The design, of course, must relate to the business it represents, and as innovations are added, they should be in context. Yet, accepting the need for suitability, the trend is to unusual designs. There is a striving for effect and less merely functional presenting of information in tradi-

2-10. Centered material results in a more classic design.

tional business-letter form. The design must be one that the user finds appropriate. It is possible to go too far with unusualness and offend a client or business prospect.

The function of the letterhead is to provide all the necessary information in readable and understandable form. This can include among other things the telex and cable addresses and any affiliated companies as well. Most importantly, it indicates to the recipient of the letter how to respond.

For one who is ordering instant printing, stationery is the simplest of assignments. All that is necessary is to present the original design in clear black and white, positioned correctly, on an 8½ × 11 inch sheet. The easiest way of doing this is simply to mount the business card in the correct position on a sheet of bond. Variety can be obtained by cutting the information apart and placing the pieces in new positions. As with the business card the same rules apply about not going too close to the edge. Since the sheet will be pre-cut and fed to the press from the end, either the top or the bottom must have approximately a ½ inch border to allow for the grippers on the press. If the image does not make this allowance, the stationery will have to be printed on an oversize sheet and trimmed.

While paper is part of the overall design and an elegant design on cheap paper might not do, most business communication really requires only the serviceable quality of paper offered by instant printers. The length of time correspondence will be kept governs how good the paper must be. Like newsprint, the cheaper papers will soon yellow and begin to crack within a few years, when exposed to air and light. Rag content paper will last longer. But kept within file fold-

2-11. With the design placed on the right the business letter may be typed with all lines starting at the left-hand margin. The required statement at the bottom balances the design.

ers, normal papers are perfectly adequate for the legal requirements of seven years specified by most business people.

Stationery is ordered separately in any quantity desired, and additional amounts can always be obtained as needed. As a general rule, letter paper is used at a rate of something like one and a half sheets to the envelope, allowing for revisions and the occasional longer letter.

Because of the availability of colored correction fluids and strikeover sheets for typing errors, there is more tendency to use colored paper for correspondence. Some people even use color on color with brown, blue, green, or red typing ribbons for an overall effect. And there are pens in colors to match.

2-12. Different sizes of envelopes are stocked by the printer. Most used is the standard number 10, seen at the top. There are also envelopes for mailings, brochures, pamphlets, billings, invoices, and return and window envelopes.

ENVELOPES for business use are generally number 10 size. These measure 9½ × 4 3/16 inches and have been universally adopted for the usual two folds of the standard letter. For business use custom places the return address in the upper left-hand corner of the envelope, the destination address in the center of the envelope, and the postage in the upper right-hand corner. The logo is included with the return address.

Some variation is possible with this arrangement, but the requirements of the post office place limits on what can be done with the design. Like a post card, the return address with logo and art should not occupy more than one half the space on the front of the envelope. The sending address and the postage must be clearly located on the other half. The stamp is required to be in the upper right-hand corner because the canceling machine runs across that area. If variations that differ radically from the custom are attempted, the only safe course is to submit the design to the post office for approval. They

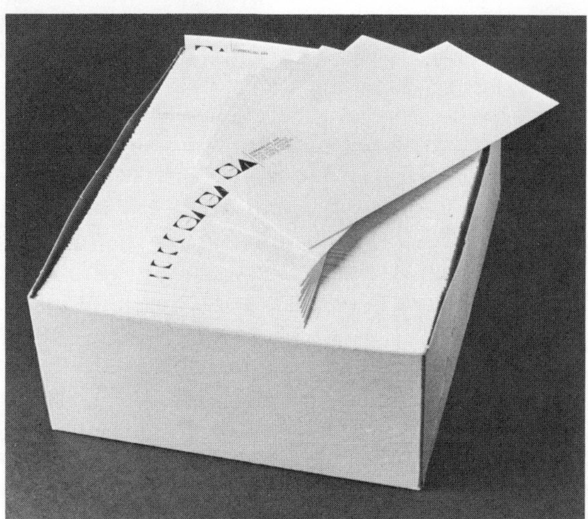

2-13. Envelopes continue the logo design. They are most economically purchased in boxes of five hundred.

2-14. The information on the envelope usually consists only of the logo and the return address. Conventional placement is in the upper left-hand corner.

2-15. Though this sideways design is more unusual, it is clear that this is the return address. In more extreme designs the sending address must always be unmistakable.

are usually very conservative.

One deviation from custom is to place the return address vertically on the left end of the envelope. In another design the return address appears below the logo, but farther down to align with the addressee. Though this risks mixing the return address with the addressee, the distinction of print from typewritten letters is usually sufficient to distinguish the two. Or a border around the return address and logo or art can act to fence the design in and separate it from the addressee. Sometimes the situation is reversed, and the addressee and postage are surrounded with a cartouche the way some designs treat the body of a business letter. Since a design is subject to so many variations, there are few rules, but the effect must be to separate the two elements so that the addressee is clearly understandable and the postage is in the required place.

It should be noted that, because the typewriter loses its grip on the envelope about an inch from the bottom, it is easier to type in the upper and middle portions of the envelope.

Baronial envelopes present an opportunity for a different kind of design because of their squarish shape. But since they are most often used for social occasions, for invitations or greetings, they are inappropriate for almost all business purposes. In any event they require that a letter be folded in two directions, and this necessitates a different set up for the instant printer's folding machine.

Use of the back flap of the envelope for the return address is also generally reserved for social correspondence. Since it is harder to feed the formed envelope with the side with the flap up, printing on the flap carries an extra charge. The instant printer will usually print the envelopes at the end of the day, and this means a day's wait.

A business card design can be used on the envelope, after removal of the phone number. If you attach your business card to the envelope as artwork, use typewriter correcting fluid to opaque the phone number.

The instant printer stocks and sells envelopes by the box of five hundred though they can be purchased in smaller quantities. The price includes printing charges. Conveniently, the paper of the envelopes matches the stationery, both in quality and color. But the use of colored papers, inks, and typewriter ribbons suggests the possibility of mixing colors, instead of using matching papers for cards, stationery, and envelopes. It suggests, for example, the possibility of using a blue typing ribbon on buff-colored paper with blue envelopes. Many other possible combinations could create colorful effects without printing in anything other than black ink.

FORMS at their best are genuine labor savers, reducing repetitive recording tasks to manageable levels. They are so much used that they are now big business, produced in wide variety and readily available. And with computer requirements for form and sequence, the use of forns is expected to quintuple in the next decade. Commercially available forms are well-designed, but they are not planned for a specific business operation or a particular company. Instant printing makes

2-16. Business reply envelopes for mailings require a permit number. The vertical bars at the top are for computer handling and sorting.

VENTURES UNLIMITED
1234 Street Address, City, State 12345

PURCHASE ORDER

TO: ____________
DATE ____________
JOB NO. ____________

DESCRIPTION

AUTHORIZED BY: ____________

2-17. A purchase order with the logo, address, and form for information is one labor-saving application of the prepared form. Some businesses use them for record keeping. A letter would serve also, but purchase orders are faster and easier, if there are many buy-outs.

personalized forms economically feasible for any small business.

The problem we all have with forms is that they either aren't specific enough or are so specific that the situation does not fit the information boxes. This happens when a form is poorly conceived with only the needs of the application in mind, not those of the user. The trick to designing usable forms, if it is a trick, is care in identifying, selecting, framing, and sequencing repetitive information. It can take a lot of thought, sometimes even trial and error to pare a form down to essentials and eliminate wasted effort.

Producing a professional form does require some artwork, mainly the mechanical drawing of delicate and carefully spaced lines. Cutting and pasting parts of existing forms can to some extent make it possible to avoid the need to hire an artist to do the job. Even with a professional to prepare the finished art for reproduction, it is essential that the form also be carefully designed by a business person, who understands the requirements. If not, it may look good, but the space allocations will not do the job.

Someone who is good with a typewriter can produce an acceptable form, even a nice-looking one, by making horizontal rules with the underscore key. Since there is no key for vertical lines, either the slash or the parenthesis must be used to create boxes and other verticals, unless they are drawn with a ruler.

If a form is to be used on the typewriter, it is important that the spaces match the line-spacing mechanism of the machine. Creating the form on the typewriter takes care of this; otherwise the lines have to be measured. There are usually six—sometimes five—typewriter lines to the inch. (Note: most copiers enlarge the copy enough to throw the line count off.)

PHONE MESSAGE

For ____________

Date __/__/__ Time ____________

R'tn Call /_7 Phone # ____________

Message: ____________

By: ____________

2-18. A typical phone message form, sized to one-quarter of an 8½ × 11 inch sheet, indicates what can be done with a typewriter. Clean appearance is largely a matter of design.

It seems the goal of every form to fit all the information onto one page. Sometimes the typewriter print is just too large for this, even a machine with elite type. One answer is to have the typewritten information reduced on a copier that provides reductions of 75 percent of original size. Then the information is pasted in the desired spaces on the form, while keeping the form the required size for normal typewriter spacing. Too much reduction will make the typewritten letters illegible, so it is sometimes better to reword and shorten than to use as much as a 60 percent reduction.

Use of typesetting makes it possible to maintain legibility, yet conserve space. A carefully prepared guide can be followed by a typesetter to obtain a professional-looking form. It can be more expensive, however, depending on the form and on how the rules are prepared. The least expensive method is to draw rules and paste up the typesetting. Another advantage of this method is that it permits designing a heading that incorporates the company logo from the letterhead.

Because the instant-printing process "sees" only the image on the paper, material for instant printing can be efficiently assembled by pasting it down. In essence, "paste-up" means simply sticking the desired image in its proper location on a piece of paper, so that it looks as you want it to appear printed. The edges of the pasted paper don't print because they don't make an image on the printing plate.

With the desired image, the paste-up can be printed on any color of paper. Forms can be glued into pads, for a nominal extra charge. When pads are made (called padding), there is the possibility of collating forms into alternating colors, for a color-coded pad. Collating also costs a little more.

2-19. The small business may use a memo form as easily as a large business. Art for the form can be made up from existing stationery.

Though the copier has in many instances taken the place of carbons in the office, pads can be conveniently used with carbon paper. A further option, but more expensive, is the use of NCR (No Carbon Required) paper, which is offered by the instant printer. A hard surface underneath the copies and a fineline ball-point pen used firmly, will produce the best copies. NCR paper presents a fresh chemical surface each time, and can be used with success for as many as five copies.

It is not necessary to order large quantities to have the labor-saving benefit of forms, when they are made up with the aid of the user's ingenuity and printed by an instant printer. This perfectly suits the requirements of most small businesses. Because of the speed with which their needs can change, large orders would soon be obsolete. This way forms that don't work as they should can be revised and updated. Professional forms, because of their fineness, must be almost completely redrawn when they are changed. A small business can accomplish something similar with a pot of rubber cement and depending on how cleverly the job is done, have a presentable form.

Because of the efficiency of specifically designed, instant-printed forms, large businesses

2-20. More type is used on the invoice than on some other forms, but much of it can be taken from existing materials, and transfer type could be used for the rest.

VENTURES UNLIMITED
1234 Street Address, City, State 12345

PURCHASE ORDER

TO: ______ DATE ______

______ JOB NO. ______

DESCRIPTION

AUTHORIZED BY: ______

VENTURES UNLIMITED

MEMO

TO: ______ DATE ______

SUBJECT: ______

FROM: ______

2-21. Forms can be combined on one sheet for printing and cutting, and this further reduces the cost for a small quantity.

2-22. A continuation of the use of the logo provides a label design for covers that protect the art. It is held in a stack with a rubber band, though it might be easier to use a small box.

also are turning to their use. It is particularly appropriate for the manufacturer, for instance, who needs shop records. This is a way to have records kept.

LABELS have a variety of business applications, but the most common one is that of an address or shipping label. Many different kinds are already available at stationery stores. The reason for creating a special one is to have the convenience and finish of a pre-printed stationery item with a unique business identity.

While a shipping label is the most obvious design, there are a number of other uses peculiar to different businesses and open to a great deal of innovation. For instance, a bookstore might have a package-wrapping label; an art studio, a seal; an accountant, a ledger heading; a repair shop, a service label; and so on into areas that are designed to act as sales aids. Because labels can be almost anything, it might be easier to think of their function. They can be used for shipping, identification, explanation, protection, decoration, and selling.

Labels have in common that they are stuck onto something else, so that the instant printing must be done on a stock with an adhesive back. Instant printers generally offer two kinds of adhesive stock, usually only in white and 8½ × 11 inches in size. One kind is a dry gum that must be wetted to make it stick; the other is a high-tack adhesive under a protective sheet, which is cracked apart, and peeled off before application. Each kind has its advantages.

Sometimes it is easy enough to use a label simply by licking the back, but because of taste and because of size, it will probably be necessary to use a sponge to wet the gum adhesive evenly. Then it may be difficult to apply it quickly and neatly to prevent curling and bubbling.

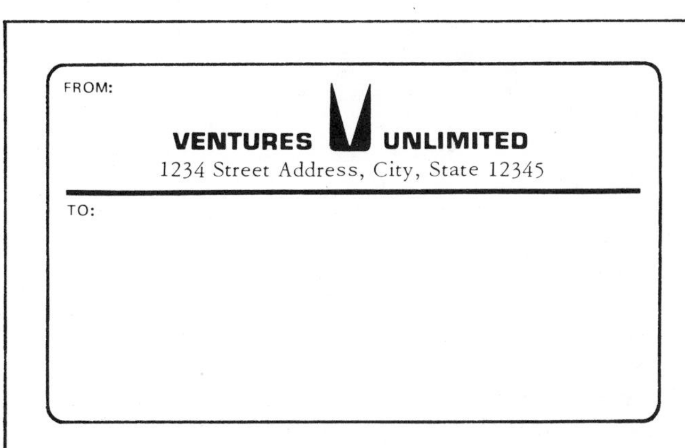

FROM:

VENTURES UNLIMITED
1234 Street Address, City, State 12345

TO:

2-23. An address label is one of the most commonly needed designs. It simplifies the work of shipping and improves the appearance of packages.

2-24. Labels are put together to make up a complete sheet for printing. They are sized to fill the sheet with room at the bottom for the press grippers.

The kind of adhesive with the protective backing may take more care in handling, but it won't curl from moisture. The label can be smoothed down as the backing is removed, so that bubbles are eliminated. It may even be pulled up again in part and restuck, if the surface it is being put on is smooth and not fibrous. This adhesive sticks easily to glass and metal as well as to paper. The scorings in the protective backing are placed on a 45 degree diagonal about 2 inches apart. While the backing can be picked off from a corner, it is much easier to bend the label to crack the score and start from the center. This would indicate a label size of approximately 2 inches square, as a minimum, so that at least one score will be on the back of each label. It is a matter of preference which kind of adhesive to use, though it seems arguable that the dry gum is better in sizes under 4 × 6 inches for sticking on paper products, and the protectively-backed adhesive is better in larger sizes on other materials as well as paper.

The range of graphic conception and design is difficult to define, so varied are the possibilities. There is, however, one factor that will not vary. We often see seals that are die-cut to the irregular shape of the design, but this is an expensive process that can only be rationalized by volume. For instant printing it is necessary to limit the shape of the label to a simple rectangle, because the printed designs will be cut apart with the trimmer, working at a square 90 degree angle. For small quantities hand trimming becomes a possibility, but any number over fifty would be a tedious project. While this is a limitation on the perimeter of the design, it does not circumscribe the graphics, since any shape can sit in a simple rectangle.

Duplicates of the design are placed together to fill up the printing area, though several different designs can be used on one sheet. It is also necessary to leave ½ inch at the end for the gripper to pull the sheet through the press. As always, it is best that borders and cartouche designs not come so close to the edge that alignment becomes a problem. The minimum is ¼ inch. Designs to be used on the typewriter should leave room for the grip between the platen and rollers of the machine to make typing manageable.

The accompanying illustrations suggest only a few possibilities of what can be done, using the logos of their respective businesses as labor savers, decorations, and sales aids. Labels come in all sizes. Personalized bumper stickers of 11 inches or even signs are possible with instant printing. To make the printed surface weather- and waterproof, brush a coat of acrylic medium or varnish over the printed-paper surface. The clear medium is approximately the same as house paint. When dry, it is waterproof, permanent, and non-yellowing.

2-25. The logo label is just big enough to use comfortably on contact adhesive stock, which has a backing to be split apart and peeled to expose the adhesive.

2-26. The logo design can be used as a package seal as well as an identity label.

2-27. A book store has a number of different applications for promotion, which would be combined to make up a sheet for printing and cutting.

2-28. Address labels are one of the many labor-saving uses of labels for a small business. Combined with others, they can be printed in suitably small quantities.

2-29. A repair label is another practical application. They can be weatherproofed with varnish.

CATALOG SHEETS might seem dull, but manufacturers need them to present information about products to the market. For the small manufacturer, accurate, up-to-date catalog sheets are called upon to carry both product information and sales. New sheets added to the catalog binder double as announcements of a new product or of changes in and additions to the product line. Retailers may have little or no need for catalog sheets, while manufacturers, operating almost entirely within an industrial environment as sub-suppliers or component manufacturers for larger concerns, make continuous use of this means of communication. Manufacturers and distributors of clothing, fast-food equipment and supplies, machine components, fasteners, and materials are examples of these kinds of small businesses. The handling and design of a catalog sheet is specialized for the flow of information, according to the many established customs within each industry.

Larger businesses have more resources and personnel to devote to communications and sales than the smaller business, which can have a difficult time getting out a good-looking catalog sheet on a limited budget. Instant printing and some of the techniques used with it are made to order for producing the sheets in limited quantity, both inexpensively and quickly.

Sales managers, who usually have the responsibility of producing catalog sheets, are making increasing use of instant-printing techniques that put together the available skills of the drafting or engineering department and the clerical or typing department.

As when people talk and make little drawings to elucidate their ideas, the explanatory catalog sheet employs art for the same purpose, and this is an area difficult for the small business to handle in-house. The problem is solved by turning to the design draftsman for a simple schematic drawing to use on the catalog sheet. Draftsmen, though not commercial artists, understand the product features well, and if the schematic drawing is limited to a size no larger than 8½ × 14 inches to fit a copier glass, it can be reduced on a copier that provides as much as a 60 percent re-

2-30. Catalog sheets for the small manufacturer can be brightened by using a preprinted form. If sufficient quantity is preprinted, color can be used economically for the design. Then for specific applications the catalog sheet information is printed over the form.

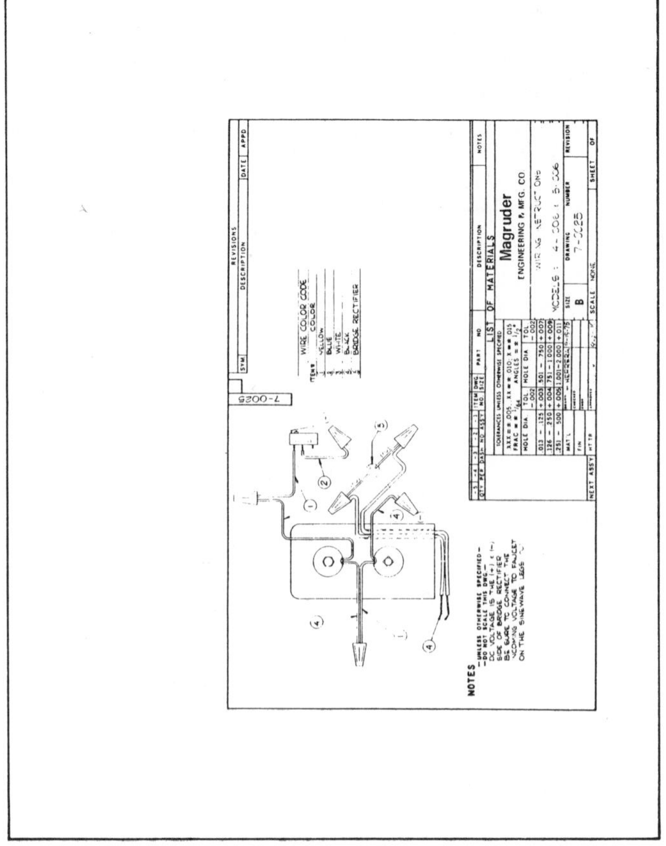

2-31. A wiring diagram is prepared by the drafting department at a size that can be copied, or reduced on a copier, and used on the catalog sheet.

duction. Full-size lettering is put on the reduction later. The copier will make the pencil lines blacker and thinner than in the original drawing, when reducing it to fit the space requirements of a standard 8½ × 11 inch catalog sheet.

Pertinent parts of engineering drawings can also be used this way, if the unwanted portions are cut off or whited out. Headings can be cut from other catalog sheets, and the remaining space filled with typewritten copy, permitting the sales manager to design and edit to fit. Then the typist will be called on to make the typewritten copy fit the space allotted to it, just as one casts a letter on letterhead stationery.

The resultant three separate pieces of paper—the reduced drawing with the lettering added, the clipped headings, and the typewritten copy—can now be assembled by pasting them on an 8½ × 11 inch sheet, so that they look just as the finished catalog sheet is to appear. The paste-up is then ready to be reproduced with instant printing.

The sales manager adapts existing skills to produce the catalog sheet and combines them through the use of the copier, paste-up, and instant printing. The same elements are used to create art professionally. In order, the sales manager substitutes the draftsman for the artist, the copier for photography, the editing for the designer, and the typist for the typesetter. As the sales manager assembles the work into paste-up, this substitutes for the printer's film stripping.

In its way, this use of instant printing parallels the traditional shortcut so familiar to many sales managers of using last year's catalog sheet for the design, using a typographer to put in the changes, and having a printer strip the new elements together with the old to produce an up-to-date sheet. Neither of these shortcuts produces the best-ever catalog sheet, though they both have gained currency and are even thriftier with instant-printing. The technique can be upgraded at all points, as needed, by improving the art preparation. Substituting type for the typewriter might be the first such upgrading; using an artist for the preparation

ASSEMBLY

1. Reconnect electrical connectors.
   Note: Index tabs permit only "one way" assembly.
2. Reapply green tape to joined connectors.
3. Insert the switch pack assembly into the housing. It may be necessary to depress the control buttons to insert and reposition it. Pull back gently to position switch pack.
4. Insert the metal wedge under the pack, with "ears" down, so that it is over indented areas in casing. Push wedge in until it is flush with the front bottom edge of the pack.
5. Pull straight back, holding case firmly. Adapter should fit snugly into assembly so screw holes line-up.
   Note: Tighten screws on each side of handle.
6. Replace two screws on side while holding adapter against case.
7. Turn power "ON."

2-32. Copy is planned and written to fit the remaining space.

Magruder ENGINEERING & MFG. CO.

Wiring Instructions

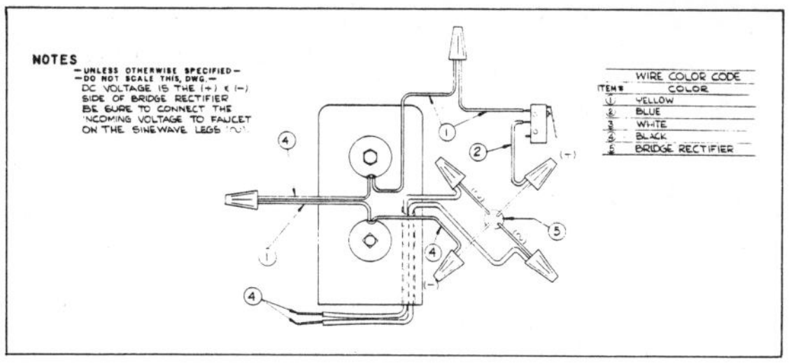

NOTES

WIRE COLOR CODE

ASSEMBLY

1. Reconnect electrical connectors.
   Note: Index tabs permit only "one way" assembly.
2. Reapply green tape to joined connectors.
3. Insert the switch pack assembly into the housing. It may be necessary to depress the control buttons to insert and reposition it. Pull back gently to position switch pack.
4. Insert the metal wedge under the pack, with "ears" down, so that it is over indented areas in casing. Push wedge in until it is flush with the front bottom edge of the pack.
5. Pull straight back, holding case firmly. Adapter should fit snugly into assembly so screw holes line-up.
   Note: Tighten screws on each side of handle.
6. Replace two screws on side while holding adapter against case.
7. Turn power "ON."

MAGRUDER ENGINEERING & MFG. CO. / 1234 BOULEVARD / CITY, STATE 12345 / (123) 456-7890 / CABLE: MGRDRCO

2-33. The pieces are pasted up in a layout that fits the space of the preprinted form. Even done simply, the results enhance the attractiveness of the catalog sheet, by providing art in an economical way.

of the paste-up, the next; incorporating photography, another.

Large concerns may also use the same techniques but with better equipment and more skills. Some use a computer plotter, word processor, or composer, and some even have a typesetting machine and graphic personnel. Each technological or craft improvement upgrades the result. A logical extension of this is the business with an in-house art department, which makes a sales manager extremely happy. An alternative is to subcontract the necessary work to an artist or typesetter to achieve the required level of quality in art preparation. For the small business, a copywriter and designer are almost unthinkable luxuries.

Because customer lists of many manufacturers, even large ones, are not big, instant printing is very desirable for the preparation of catalog sheets. It is quick and economical, and handles anything, including art and photographs, if prepared correctly.

Many manufacturers continually redesign old products and develop new ones. The research and development department is in continuous operation, making running changes. There is no model year as such, with the result that there is a constant need for development and revision of catalog sheets to supply the customer list.

Ring binders or other looseleaf holders are needed to hold the manufacturer's catalog, so that the constant flow of changes can be accommodated, and instant printing is often the best way to keep up with them. Catalog sheets keep the designer, fabricator, and retailer up-to-date on the manufacturing market.

2-34. Sheets for clipping that include much-used art, such as different sizes of logos, are useful for preparing catalog sheets quickly and easily.

FLIERS are used to put the retailer in direct touch with his customers. Like handbills, they are among the oldest forms of advertising, the difference between them being that handbills are passed out by hand to moving foot traffic, while fliers are distributed in any number of different ways. Depending on the business, fliers can be passed out from a counter display; they can be carried through the community served by the retailer; they can be mailed; and they can be handed out. Fliers sent through the mail conform to the uses of direct-mail advertising.

They make the same kind of connection with the market for the retailer that catalog sheets make for the manufacturer, but they must direct a stronger advertising appeal to customers. Since the largest share of small business works to service a locality or community, the flier is employed to increase foot traffic to the store. Fliers can't sell anything really, but they can start a process with a potential customer, which may result in a sale.

To accomplish the flier's purpose of selling the small retail business and its services to the community various products or benefits are offered. As with all advertising there must be something to appeal to the interest of the customer and sufficient information for the customer to take action. All kinds of small retail businesses can use fliers. Service businesses, such as repair shops, have one kind of use for a flier, while a goods retailer has another. A special interest business, focusing on particular activities, like sports or hobbies, will have a different kind of flier that appeals more to activity than to service.

As newspapers serve an area, fliers work in a similar way, but with more focused distribution and lower cost. Presumably, the flier will reach only those who are potential customers, while the wider circulation of the newspaper would perhaps be wasted on those beyond the range of the business. But producing a flier is rather like producing a newspaper ad, something most buyers and small business operators are familiar with. The major differences between an ad and a flier are that the flier need not compete for attention with other ads in a given space, and because of this can take almost any appropriate graphic treatment from slick to homespun.

Sometimes for the small retailer the flier's construction is more difficult than the content, since most business owners are trained to deal with content, but not with the graphic possibilities available for their use.

But like a letterhead, instant printing a flier is as simple and inexpensive as presenting a one-sheet design to the printer. If necessary, both sides of the sheet can be used, with each side re-

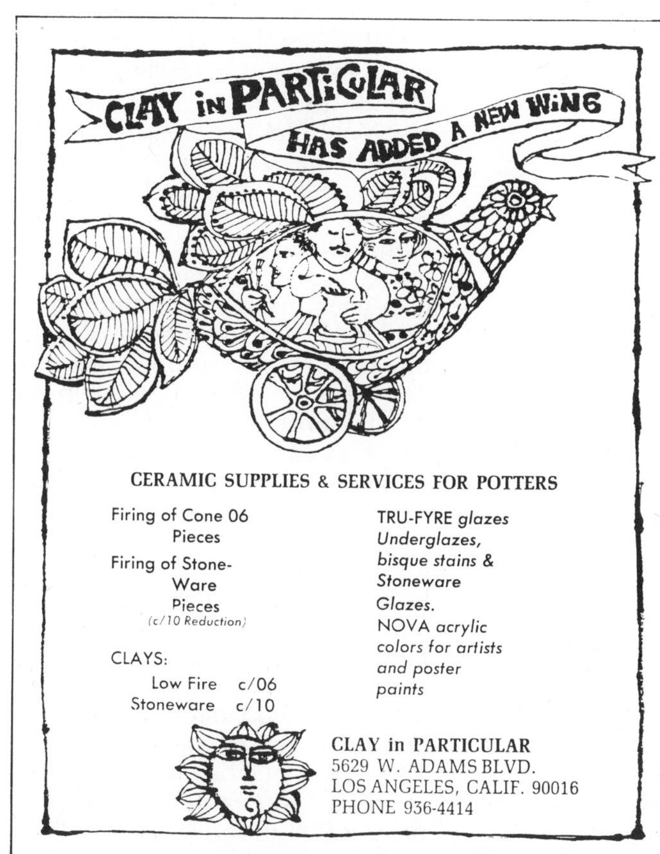

2-35. Preparing a flier for a retail business is like doing a retail newspaper ad. Here a connection is made between copy and art that has a nice balance of casualness and expertise.

2-36. Salad lovers must like greenery, and the well-done art and limited copy provide a strong appeal with outstanding simplicity.

quiring its own paste-up. Colored paper can be utilized effectively not only as an aid to the design but also as an identity factor in later repeated efforts. All that is needed is to assemble the material and paste it onto a sheet of paper for duplication with instant printing. Even the typewriter can be pressed into action to complete the message, though most retailers have letterheads and other materials that can be used along with pictures often supplied by the manufacturer of the product.

Flyer
8½ x 11

Flyer
8½ x 14

2-38. Fliers can be done conveniently in each of these three instant printing format sizes. By far the most used is the 8½ × 11 inch format.

Manufacturers sometimes make promotional materials available to the retailer for advertising, and these can be helpful in the production of fliers. With the newspaper's permission parts of the proof of an ad may be reusable. Transfer art and clip art also come in handy.

Preparation of material is similar to that of the catalog sheet though the sources are different. The retailer has many more possibilities for the 8½ × 11 inch sheet than the manufacturer. Transfer type is very popular for the do-it-yourself flier. More elaborate designs can be created with the help of an artist to assemble the material and make drawings.

If photographs are used, they should be screened, as is done in a newspaper, because unscreened photos will not reproduce properly. Be sure that the graphic material used is not copyrighted and may be used, because the owner of the material can sue and collect if you violate his rights.

Manufacturer's clip art is the easiest to use, and the local newspaper might be willing to provide it for advertisers. The instant printer may have such a convenience for his customers. Clip art can also be found in an art store with transfer type or in books for this purpose. And a number of studios supply clip art by mail order.

A coupon or free offer is the only way to check the actual effectiveness of a one-sheet flier. A return of two percent is considered average for a direct mail response, and as all advertisers learn there is generally not an immediate response to their appeals. It is the cumulative effect of a sustained effort that has a greater result in fostering public awareness of a business activity.

The popularity of fliers is proof of their serviceability. They remain a very basic form of advertising communication for the small business.

2-37. Done almost entirely with drawing, this flier indicates the many applications that fliers can be put to. Part of its effectiveness is its original 11 × 17 inch size.

PAMPHLETS consist of a few sheets or are composed of one folded sheet. You don't often hear about leaflets anymore. Now when the item contains perhaps eight to a dozen sheets or more, it is called a booklet. A brochure is a more elaborate booklet, usually larger and containing a greater emphasis on illustration. But the terms pamphlet, leaflet, booklet, and brochure are not precise and may be used interchangeably in a more general sense. They all usually contain typeset material.

2-39. Booklets or pamphlets of many different sizes can be made with the three instant printing formats by different folds or by cutting the sheet in half after printing two at a time.

The difference between a pamphlet and a flier is in the folding. The material printed in a pamphlet is arranged to correspond to the folds, while the material on a flier is designed to fill one sheet only.

A pamphlet is printed on both sides in all but rare cases. Depending on the design of the folds and the amount of illustration, the pamphlet is conceived of as having a preponderance of printed matter, organized to the folds even when fully opened. If the material opens out in successively larger folds to a full-sheet display, it may be called a broadside, though again this term is subject to different interpretations. A broadside is usually large, at least 24 inches.

For instant printing the sheet size is limited to 11 × 17 inches. The 8½ × 14 inch legal size sheet makes a pamphlet when folded in half and then in half again. This provides four sections on each side for print matter, so that the text is set in columns that run in the 8½ inch direction. The standard 8½ × 11 inch sheet can be made into a pamphlet of two folds, as is done for a business letter but with the text in columns in each of the three sections. With the different folds possible in the three sizes, a fair number of designs can be created to make up a pamphlet. The design of the pamphlet would depend on the amount of the text, the art, and the requirements for display. It would be normal, for instance, that the topmost fold be used as

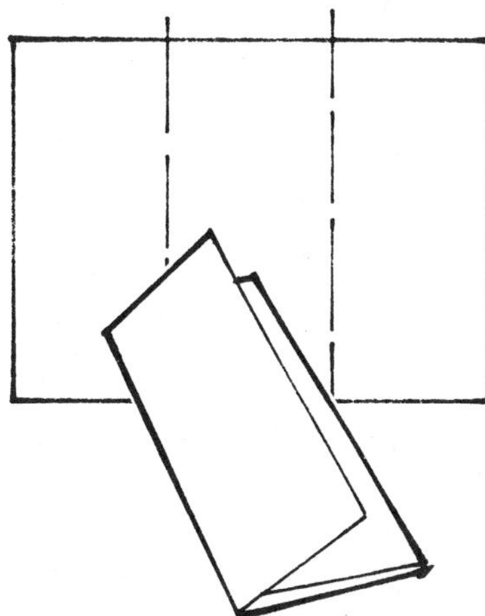

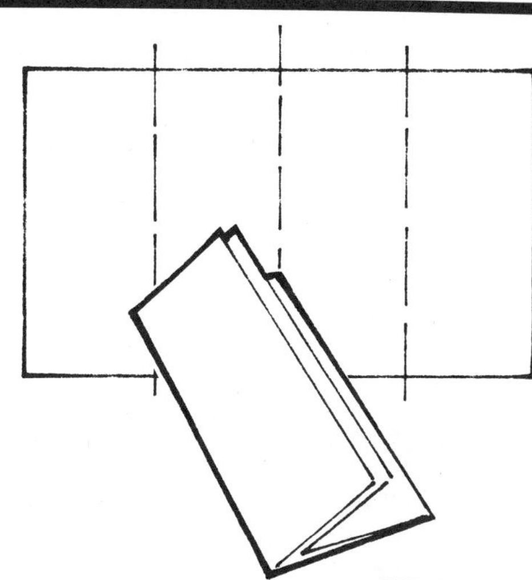

2-40. The two most popular pamphlet sizes are made from the 8½ × 11 inch and the 8½ × 14 inch instant printing formats.

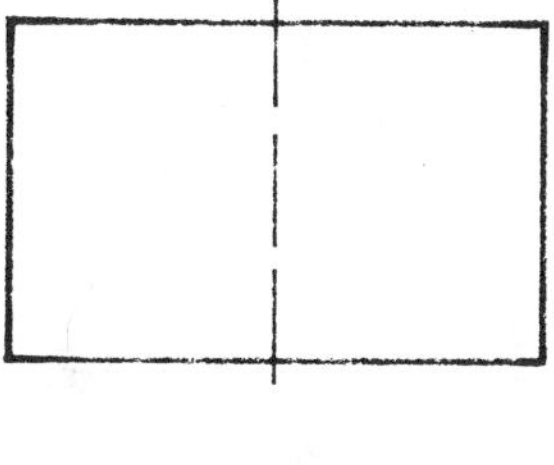

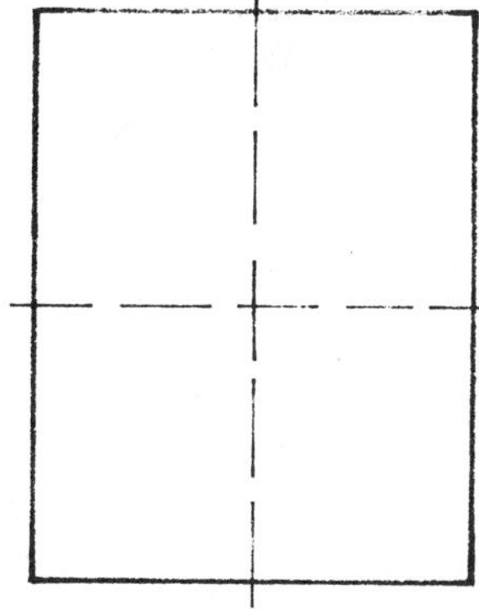

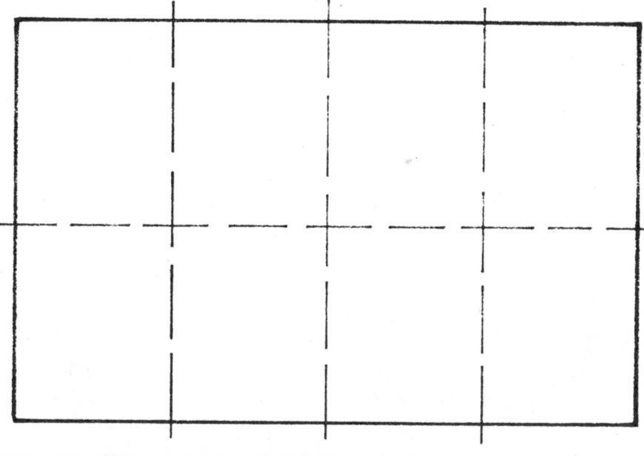

2-41. The broadside starts with the smallest size showing and then successively doubles its size to the format of 17 × 11 inches or used the other way, to 11 × 17 inches.

a cover for the title with perhaps some art.

A booklet can be made of the pamphlet by binding it with staples and then trimming the edges to free each leaf or page. For instance, the 8½ × 14 inch sheet folded in half twice, then stapled at the center fold, can be trimmed at the outside edge to make an eight-page booklet. Two sheets stapled and folded this way can produce a sixteen-page booklet. When the pamphlet is expanded into a booklet, consideration must be given to the size and weight and to the general feel of the booklet. With only a few pages it can be attractive to use a heavier stock for the outside cover to prevent the booklet from bending at the spine when folded and stapled. These considerations and the amount of material govern the design of the folds, the size and number of pages, and the format of the booklet.

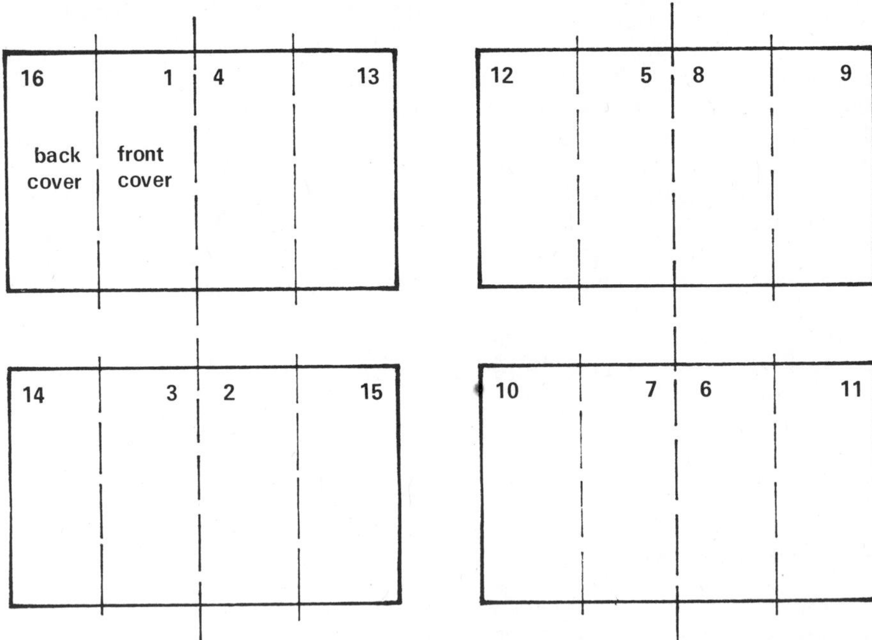

2-42. When two 8 ½ × 14 inch sheets are gathered inside each other, stapled, and trimmed to make up a booklet, the page numbering falls this way on front and back. It is difficult to visualize without making a dummy and numbering the pages.

A prime consideration for a pamphlet or booklet is the style and use of text. Elegant typewriter type might be used, but the preparation of a booklet often requires typesetting. Conventional designs require justified type, in which both the right-hand and left-hand margins are held to a straight line. It is possible to do justified typing, but the narrow columns of a conventional pamphlet or booklet leave less space than usual for typing. On average, typesetting takes approximately 40 percent less space than the typewriter for the same legibility. The greater expense of printing, folding, gathering, stapling, and trimming a booklet may warrant the idea of typesetting the text. Coupled with the fact that typesetting takes less space, typesetting could save an extra sheet and almost pay for itself.

If the typewriter is used to make a booklet, larger sheet sizes are easier. One of the preferred sizes is the 8½ × 14 inch sheet folded in half and stapled at the fold. Its size is then 7 × 8½ inches.

The array of formats and variety of design might well call for help from an artist, when some of the more complex designs are attempted or when the material in the pamphlet or booklet is complicated. Simple formats, however, should be within reach of most. Booklets and pamphlets in any number of different formats can be done with instant printing, and as the folds and the trimmer are brought into the process, the variety of possibilities increases. Through instant printing, small quantities can be produced at a feasible price, as compared with the volume necessary to rationalize job printing. With really small volume, the originator can even do some work by hand—gathering, stapling, or folding—further reducing the cost of producing a pamphlet or booklet.

To assemble the design for a booklet it is essential to make up a dummy, or model, to see where the pages will fall on the front and back of the printed sheets. When the pages are pasted up for printing, they probably will not appear in the order they will have when they are assembled and bound. It is very easy to make a mistake in positioning pages, and making a dummy is the best way to check for accuracy. When the booklet dummy is taken apart, the pages will be positioned correctly.

Different colored paper may be used to advantage for the cover and sometimes for an interior page, according to the design. While the originator will have to supply the material in finished form, the instant printer will help with the organization, since it is he who will handle the actual assembly of the booklet.

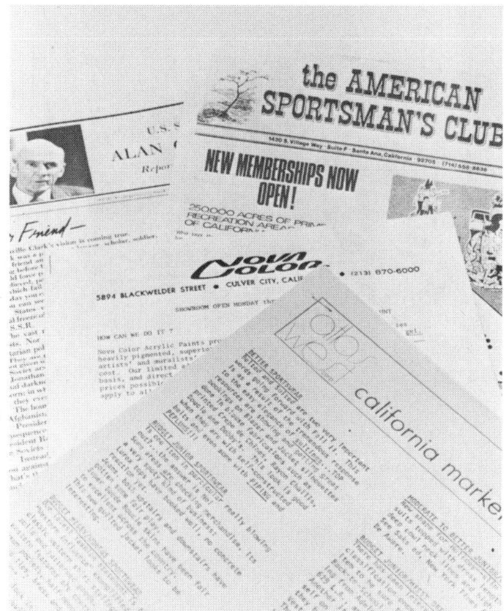

2-43. Instant printing may well have contributed to the increasing popularity of newsletters, because it provides an inexpensive way to produce them for limited distribution. This small sampling shows the various ways they are used by all kinds of organizations.

DESIGNER'S NEWSLETTER o 1234 STREET NAME o CITY NAME, STATE NAME 1234 o PHONE (123) 456-7890

Designer's Newsletter

DESIGNER'S NEWSLETTER COPYRIGHT 1984. All rights reserved. No portion may be reproduced by any means.

2-44. Newsletters have in common a heading treatment that identifies the purpose or organization. Because it is a form that repeats, it could be preprinted in color.

NEWSLETTERS, used by business to boost morale, to inform and unify, to communicate and coordinate, continue to grow in popularity through the use of instant printing. So diverse are the uses of newsletters that they are put out by individuals, groups, interests, and foundations as well as businesses. Newsletters range from simplified publications at one extreme to virtual slick magazines at the other. It is the simple communication of a letter expanded in a variety of forms, the design depending to some extent on the subject matter and on the purpose of the communication.

The most common kind is done on typewriter on an 8½ × 11 inch sheet with heading and paragraph treatment distinguishing each item of news. Symbols, like the asterisk, the underscore, or the number sign, are sometimes used as an additional treatment for more definition or to characterize different kinds of units, such as lead-ins, headings, or endings. In comparison with an ordinary typewritten letter, the typed layout is especially well done. As the amount of information in the publication grows, it may run to several pages. Next, the design can be printed on a four-page 17 × 11 inch sheet and be paginated.

The stationery heading of the organization adds to the effectiveness and appearance of the newsletter. Two-color designs are often used, and preprinted sheets can include a banner, logo and heading, organizational statements, officers, and a floor line. The use of preprinted sheets is like doing instant printing on preprinted stationery, and in large volume it saves money. The sheets are then used later with instant printing at the volume of the newsletter. Any printing in color is always less expensive per unit, when done in volume rather than at the smaller quantity of the newsletter.

Use of instant printing lowers the cost of a newsletter when the quantities are in the range of sev-

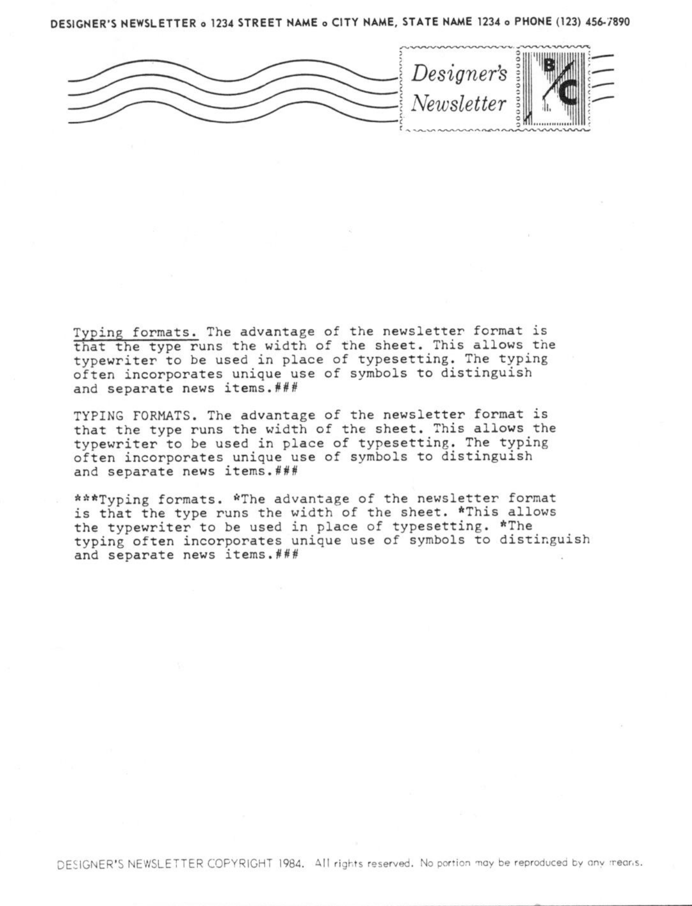

DESIGNER'S NEWSLETTER o 1234 STREET NAME o CITY NAME, STATE NAME 1234 o PHONE (123) 456-7890

Designer's Newsletter

Typing formats. The advantage of the newsletter format is that the type runs the width of the sheet. This allows the typewriter to be used in place of typesetting. The typing often incorporates unique use of symbols to distinguish and separate news items.###

TYPING FORMATS. The advantage of the newsletter format is that the type runs the width of the sheet. This allows the typewriter to be used in place of typesetting. The typing often incorporates unique use of symbols to distinguish and separate news items.###

***Typing formats. *The advantage of the newsletter format is that the type runs the width of the sheet. *This allows the typewriter to be used in place of typesetting. *The typing often incorporates unique use of symbols to distinguish and separate news items.###

DESIGNER'S NEWSLETTER COPYRIGHT 1984. All rights reserved. No portion may be reproduced by any means.

2-45. The typing of newsletters is carefully thought out. The biggest distinction between newsletters is the use of either typing or typesetting, which is often done to conserve space.

2-46, 2-47. A velox, or screened halftone, is necessary when printing a photograph. If a photo is mounted in the paste-up without being screened, the printing process resolves the greys into print or no-print with this result. Depending on the tones, this black or white treatment can sometimes be used for a special effect.

eral hundred, and this makes a newsletter practical for the business needing only a small number of copies. There is not such a mechanical cost for production that the cost would suggest producing a newsletter by the thousands. Preprinted sheets simply enhance this saving, though the additional cost of designing and producing the preprinted sheets to be used with instant printing must be included.

As the newsletter expands to six pages, an 8½ × 11 inch sheet is inserted between the folded 17 × 11 inch sheet. The next size up is two 17 × 11 inch sheets folded together, a popular newsletter size. Inceasing pages beyond this point may make it advisable to use typesetting rather than the typewriter to conserve space. A four-page, typeset newsletter contains nearly as much material as an eight-page, typewritten newsletter. The quantity of the printing determines the cost and whether to go to typesetting. By using typesetting the page can be divided into columns, and often a design like that of a newspaper is preferred. The type can be set in different sizes, and several different levels of headings can be used. The newsletter, like a miniature newspaper, can even have continuations of the stories on back pages to allow for a front-page display.

Pictures may be used, if they are screened for printing. A method favored for its low cost is the use of an instant camera and then a scanner to produce an 85-line screen halftone. The halftone is pasted into position along with the type for instant printing.

With typesetting, paste-up, and the inclusion of halftone pictures, the newsletter is now being handled in nearly the same way as a newspaper. All that need be added are rules and features. Illustrations for features and headings can be obtained from clip art.

The distinction between doing art for instant printing and for conventional job printing is that all the material for instant printing must be done as line art and be sized and positioned. Since instant printing is a direct process, there is no halftone screen to turn the unprintable continuous tone of a photograph into the printable dots of a halftone screen, and no separate sizing or repositioning is possible.

A halftone scanner is rather like the imaging system used by several manufacturers of machines for telephone transmission of a graphic image. It uses a low-power laser light to make the halftone dots directly on paper as the photo is scanned. The result is exactly the same as the conventional photographic halftone process that first exposes a high-contrast negative through a screen to break the light into dots, which are then printed onto paper. The scanner produces the dots directly and avoids the negative, and because it saves labor and material, it is somewhat less expensive. Once a photograph has been screened, it is in effect line art. The tiny black dots are the same black and white art as typesetting, although the smallness and closeness of the dots make them seem to the naked eye like a gray tone. This means that any printed halftone can be reprinted with instant printing, provided the dots are not so tiny that the process cannot handle them. The 150-line screen, usually seen in fine offset-printed brochures, is too fine to be handled by instant-printing film.

In the many variations of newsletter design and makeup, whether done by typewriter, typesetting, or including art, the emphasis is always on written news more than on graphic display, and the format is characterized by its simplicity. Though conceptions of newsletter design cover a broad range of graphic treatment, they never compete with the format of a magazine or a brochure, because the intent is different. For the newsletter handling the perishable commodity of news simplicity is the watchword and instant printing extremely convenient.

COUPONS and items like certificates and counter cards can be economically prepared for the small business with instant printing. Because these products are usually never needed in great quantity, they used almost always to be too expensive for the small business to obtain.

Items such as these are usually distinguished by designs with headings, elaborate borders, ornate lettering, spaghetti-like flourishes, and outlined shapes with decoration called cartouches. Coupons, for instance, are so often done with a border that it serves almost as identification. The art is, therefore, more elaborate for these products than for most produced with instant printing. A good deal of time and thought is required for their preparation, possibly even the services of an artist, but their promotional value in sales is easily great enough to justify the effort.

2-48. Small businesses may now do what large ones do by means of instant printing, though they require only small quantities. Counter cards are similar to coupons, and a coffee shop set up may include an ad for the day's special.

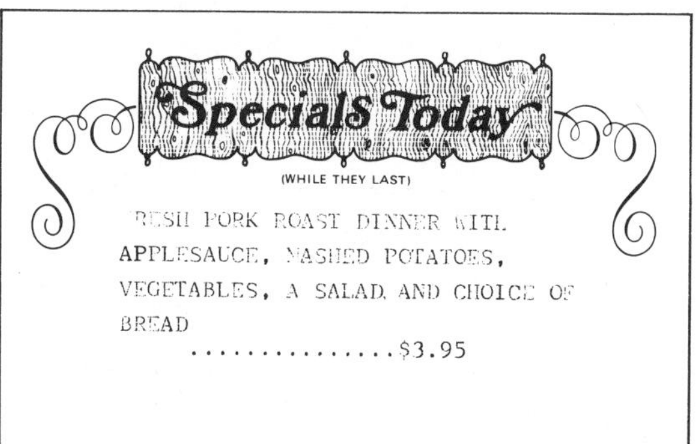

2-49. Art for a counter card is decorative, anything that fits the purpose.

Gift Certificate

Mostly Books
4016 Wilshire Boulevard
Los Angeles, CA 90010

Mostly Books

will redeem this certificate for merchandise

in the amount of ____________

To ____________

From ____________ Date ____________

Address ____________

By ____________
Authorized By

2-50. The retailer's gift certificate is another occasion when only a small quantity is needed. If the art is too complicated for the neophyte, it might be worthwhile hiring an artist.

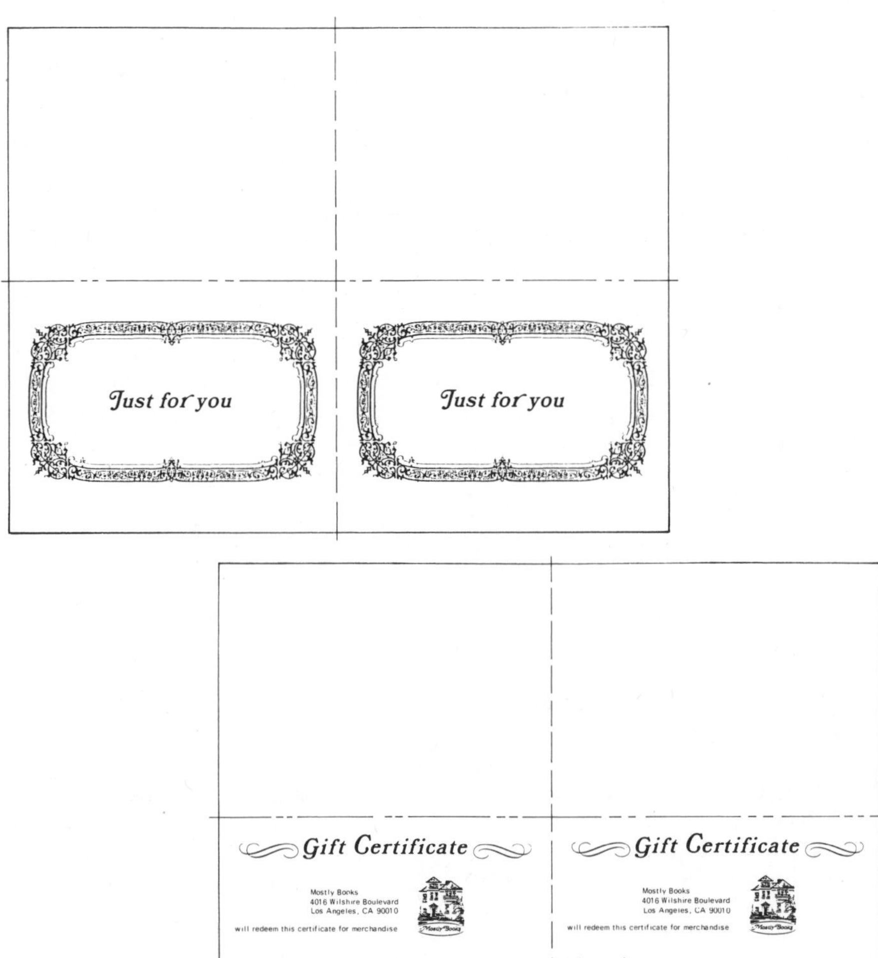

2-51, 2-52. One kind of gift certificate design has two sides, folding over to make a gift card. It prints two at a time in the 8½ × 11 inch format on index stock and is cut apart.

Fortunately, with transfer type and artist's aids, there is prepared art that can be assembled to create a design. Manufacturers of transfer type offer sheets of decorative designs, including border designs, cartouche shapes, calligraphic flourishes, and other useful decorations. This is so much easier than having to draw the art from scratch that many artists use it. Because of their popularity these sheets of transfer art are available at art supply stores and at many stationers as well.

Since these designs are somewhat involved, it is best to make a small sketch first, before undertaking to assemble it. Although with artist's aids no real drawing is necessary, the arrangement of the design and the spacing of the items must be carefully done. Before starting to transfer the art to the paper, it is helpful to have a guideline for position. A pale blue pencil is useful for this purpose, obtainable at an art or stationery store. Pale blue, visible while you position the art, cannot be picked up in the reproduction process. This means that the construction lines may be left in place, an advantage, because it is very hard to clean them up without disturbing transfer type or art. With the design planned and non-reproducing blue lines in place, the transfer art is burnished onto the paper that will become the art. Instructions for this operation are provided by the different manufacturers.

Once the transfer art and type are in place, the various other elements are added. Perhaps clip art and copy are included and must be pasted down to complete the design. Because of the number of steps involved, this may sound complicated, but a design can be done simply. A coupon can be made up with just a border design, and clean, good-looking typewriter type. If the offer is effective, the coupon will be too.

The illustration at the top of page 31 shows just such a simple coupon. It is first printed to copy it, making enough duplicates to assemble the paste-up for the 8½ × 11 inch sheet used for printing. With such a fine-line design it is probably better to use instant printing for the copying. If a copier is used, it will usually show the faint blue construction lines, because the copier is not an orthochromatic process. The construction lines will then have to be opaqued on each duplicate. There is no absolute necessity to make the coupon fit exactly with no waste of printing paper. A coupon or any other item can be of any convenient size to be assembled to print in multiples with the least amount of waste. A multiple of a design can sometimes fit the 8½ × 14 inch size better, depending on the shape of the design.

Gift certificates and counter cards can be handled in a similar fashion. The more elaborate the design, the more difficult the art, but that is up to the discretion of the innovator.

A small amount of type for

2-53. A coupon design with a relatively simple treatment but an irresistible offer is bound to succeed. This is obviously not a big print run, but it is a tried and proven way to build business.

the copy portion (not the heading) can usually be set for a minimum price, if it is felt that the typewriter would not have the right appearance. To get type, first type up the copy exactly as it is wanted; then take the typewritten copy and the design to a typesetter, who will set it to the size and space wanted.

Some counter cards are designed with the use of a typewriter in mind. The design shown fits a holder and displays the special of the day.

More complicated designs like awards or diplomas can be undertaken if there is someone who can do the calligraphic lettering for the names. Just a few names could be handled with transfer type that looks like the Gothic style used in calligraphy. Some instant printers stock parchment paper, and it can be used for effect. For diplomas, the seal would be obtained through a stationery store.

Satisfaction cards, complaint cards, and guarantees can likewise be included in this group of products. The complexity of the design will depend on the skill of the person assembling it. Designs that require delicate proportions, ruled lines, and a considerable amount of paste-up may best be given to an artist, but a typesetter can sometimes do a number of setups that allow a talented novice to turn complicated elements into aesthetically pleasing designs.

2-54. The coupons are placed together, run, and then cut apart. Sheets of paper could be of different colors, distributed in different areas to see where business originates.

PERSONAL PRODUCTS

Stationery and department stores are crowded with printed products that we all use, from note pads to wrapping paper. But they are necessarily designed and mass-produced for the widest possible market. Now—through instant printing—these items can be individualized, opening a channel for personal expression. The users become their own inventors and designers, crafting products to fit their own tastes and requirements. Also feasible are gifts with a custom touch. And all this is possible in small quantities at a reasonable cost. The following products should serve to suggest a great variety of possibilities for the innovative user.

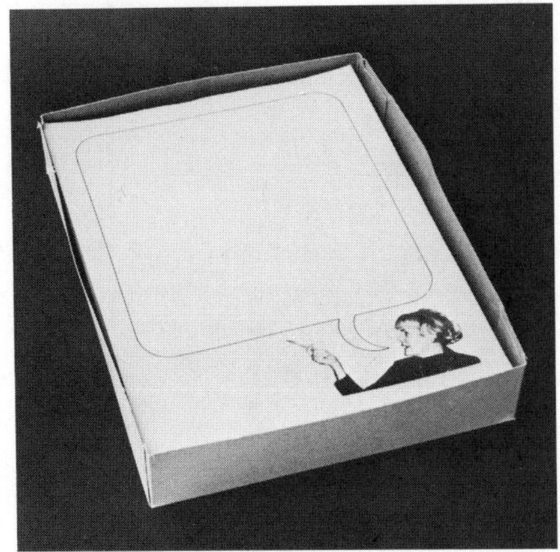

2-55. Products for yourself can be printed in small quantities. A full ream of five hundred sheets may seem like too many, but they seem to disappear.

NOTEPAPER is needed by everyone for correspondence with friends, for thank-you's, condolences, and invitations. It is more often informal than formal, and though the formal needs to be neat and tailored, the informal can follow almost any design.

Formal notepaper often incorporates monograms, crests, family emblems, or mottoes. Since commercial products cannot be personalized with family insignia or heraldry, notepaper in the United States has tended to the more informal. But any design can be made more rigid and formal through the use of symmetry and centering.

Informal notepaper, often asymmetrical, can be decorative, humorous, elegant, catchy, simple, or whatever is desired. Decoration and motif can say anything the user wants. The wide range of invention provides for an element of fun, and within the bounds of taste, witty sayings and cartoons are possible. The

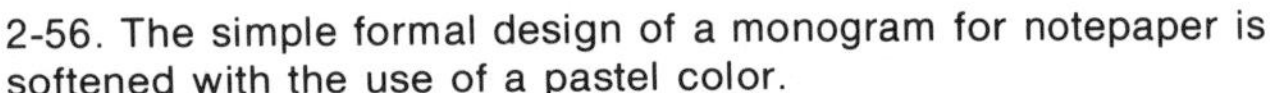

2-56. The simple formal design of a monogram for notepaper is softened with the use of a pastel color.

2-57. Informal notepaper design has many uses. A picture is a clever idea and says it all.

underlying purpose of notepaper is to decorate and identify a communication.

On notepaper one assumes the conventional form of presentation, with the decoration not encroaching upon the spaces usually used for salutation, message, and signature. Since instant printing, however, allows the user to personalize, it is completely possible to devise an individual form for the conventional elements, just so long as the necessary information is there for the recipient. Even commercial notepaper can be personalized.

Though some people might feel hesitant, it is fun to draw your own design. The non-artist may copy, trace, photograph, and clip designs. It is simple enough to trace over another drawing, making changes, for the simple act of tracing will show that it is impossible really to copy anything done by another. No two individuals move their hands the same way. The end result always reveals differences. Such improvisation should serve to initiate a completely new, personal design.

The law allows the use of a copier to reproduce pages from a copyrighted book in a public library, but adopting another's design for personal use would stretch the copyright law out of all recognition. It would be a better idea, and more fun, to purchase art prepared for transfer or clipping. It is possible even to add one's own flourishes to the design with a pen.

Much thought can be given to sayings, epigrams, or proverbs that dispense wit and wisdom. It is the thought that counts, though how you say it has a lot to do with the way it is received. If sayings are not too long, they can be put down with transfer type. Otherwise the use of a typewriter or typesetting gives a finished look to the art. Typewriter material reduced by a copier can be effective.

Photos must be screened before they can be reproduced with any fidelity to their normal tonal appearance. It requires a halftone photoprint that makes the toned area into very small dots. This is the opportunity to change the size of the photo to whatever is required by the design. Once the design is worked out it will be pasted down on a sheet that indicates the size wanted. All the "camera copy" has to be black and white to be reproducible.

If convenient, it is also possible to do the paste-up in a larger size than wanted, then have it reduced to the proper dimensions for printing. Do not make the art larger than double size, and do not include halftones because the change in size will alter the density of the halftone screen, making the dots even smaller.

The size of the notepaper can be varied. Though 8½ × 11 inches is a standard size, notepaper can also be done in half sheets of 5½ × 8½ inches, or it can be done in the standard 8½ × 11 size but folded in half to provide four sides, front and back, or only two sheets, front and front, depending on the thickness of the paper used.

Printing is a straightforward use of instant printing and can be done on colored papers, which may also be mixed. Another possibility is to print a small quantity of several different designs with various messages for various purposes. For smaller size notepaper printing the design in twos would require duplicating it and placing the pair side by side on the 8½ × 11 inch sheet to be

2-58. A well-known cat personality is expressed by his owner's illustrations on this half-sheet size notepaper. K. C. stands for Kitty Cat.

trimmed apart later. Printing in twos also provides space for different designs. Folding is normally done by the letter writer as each sheet is used. When notepaper is done with folds or in sizes smaller than the 8½ × 11 inch format, it will naturally require a different size envelope.

2-59. Note cards use many kinds of art and a variety of different styles to reflect the feelings of the sender.

NOTE CARDS perform the same variety of functions as notepaper. The emphasis, though, is on art, with the format providing one panel for a picture, another for a short message. Some people use three of the four panels for writing. In the selection of a picture for the cover panel the innovative user makes a personal statement. The Sunday artist can do a painting, for example. Personalized, formal note cards may bear the family insignia. The black and white art of a pen-and-ink drawing reproduces nicely. It can be done at the same size it will be used or larger to be reduced by a copier or photostat. A painting can be shot photographically, then sized and cropped when the screened photoprint is made so that it fits the note card format.

It is harder to assemble suitable art for a note card by using only clip art and transfer art. Such art is purposely designed to be appropriate for the greatest number of users, and the note card should be open to a more distinctive and interpretive statement.

One very satisfactory way for the non-artist to obtain a drawing is to commission an artist to do one. This need not be an expensive undertaking, but depending on the character of the art, it should be unique and effective.

Another way to decorate the front of a note card is to find and reuse art that is out of copyright. This course often yields stylish antiques of quaint and charming character. Sometimes children's books from the late nineteenth century often have wonderful drawings done in the black-and-white art so popular at that time. Work created prior to 1900 is out of copyright and safe to use. Sometimes antique labels or containers, also well out of copyright, can provide art for a personal note card, as can old catalogs or periodicals. These of course would be prepared for reproduction with photography and a halftone screen or by making a photostatic copy of line art.

Antique art is a rich source, but it is not quite so easy as it sounds because the would-be note card designer must see the art with fresh eyes and be able to

2-60. Original paintings can be photographed for a note card. Raggedy Ann cards are packaged as a gift.

2-61. Different Raggedy Ann designs can be paired for printing side by side on index stock. Photos need to be veloxed.

2-62. A rose note card design has many uses. Another type of design could be printed alongside.

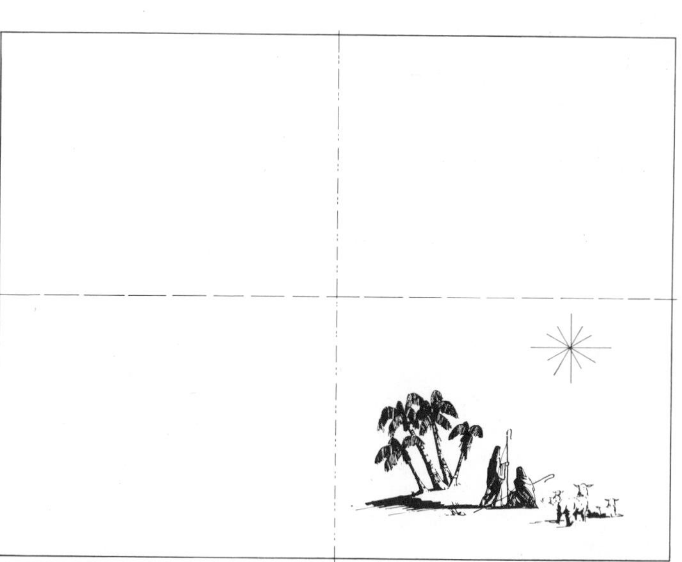

2-63. Christmas cards can be done in the same format. Since this design is horizontal, a card on the opposite side of the sheet would have to be also. Either direction for the design would use the same envelope.

envision it as it would be interpreted on a notecard. It is sometimes necessary to eliminate small portions or to make a new frame to display it. The succesful note card illustration is one that provides just the right flavor. The attraction one feels to the art is often subjective, and for this reason unique and quixotic drawings often work surprisingly well.

Again, a paste-up of the art needs to be supplied for instant-printing. Since note cards take up only a portion of the space on an 8½ × 11 inch sheet, it is often convenient to print two different designs side by side or to duplicate a design and print it twice. Note cards can be made smaller than 4¼ × 5½ inches, but this size is popular because it is one-half of a folded 8½ × 11 inch sheet, and it fits a 5¾ × 4 7/16 inch baronial envelope, which many instant printers supply. After printing, the 8½ × 11 inch sheet is trimmed in half.

Normally note cards are printed on the index card stock supplied by the instant printer. It will be heavy enough for the size suggested but no larger. Bigger sizes need a heavier board for the note card to have the desirable stiffness.

Of course, note cards can be done in other than a conventional format with art on one, two, or three panels of an 8½ × 11 inch, two-fold design that fits a standard business envelope. Such a design with art on just two panels can become a self-mailer, not requiring an envelope. In this case the address is on the third panel and the message on the inside of the card. But personal note cards often have the printing limited to the outside, which makes up the front and back panels of the note card when folded. The two inside blank panels are used for the message.

2-64. This Christmas card design uses the entire sheet and requires an oversize envelope.

Though the question is more pertinent to a greeting card than to a note card, there is sometimes a need to have printing on both sides of the sheet. The answer is either to print on both sides or to use a French fold. This is usually done on heavy paper, not on index board. It is folded in half on the 11 inch length with the printing to the outside. Then, as with the customary note card or greeting card, it is folded again in the other direction. This places what becomes the inside of the card on the same surface as the cover, so it can be printed at the same time as the cover. Be careful to make up a dummy of a card with the French fold, so that the paste-up of the design is correctly positioned in the quadrants, head to head or side to side. The relationship of the positions is deceptive.

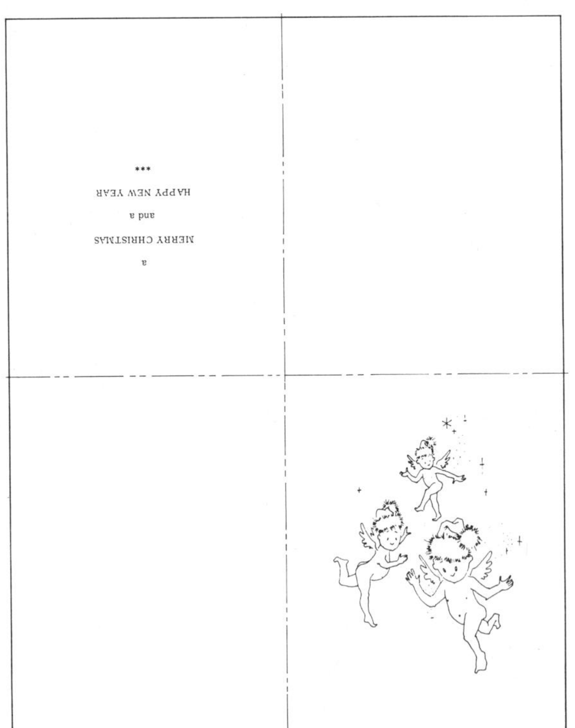

2-65. The French fold uses the entire sheet. By folding in half lengthwise and then in half again the other way, the message arrives on the inside. A cherub or angel design would be good all year round, but Santa hats turn it into a Christmas design.

Index stock is often available in colors, and these can be chosen with a view to the effect on the art and the color of ink to be used in writing the message. Pens with various inks are available for an attractive color scheme on note cards, without resorting to printing in anything but black ink. Printing can be done in color as well, but at an additional cost.

Nevertheless, when the art is as important as it is on a note card, it may be worthwhile to use a second color against the black. One easy use of a second color can be for a border or background. To make the art for the second color use a piece of tracing paper and a black pen and fill in those areas you wish to print in color. Be sure to mark the corners of the sheet so that the color can be positioned as you intended. Also, do not place the color directly at the edges of the art to be printed in black, because press technology cannot match the position that accurately. When color is used, design it to float in the position you indicate on the tracing paper. The tracing paper is then photographed as an original paste-up and positioned to print according to the corner marks.

Sometimes an effect of color, without the cost, can be obtained by adding tone to black-and-white art through use of a self-adhesive transfer sheet obtained at an art supply store. The tone, which is really made up of very fine black and white dots, is placed on or around the art, and can be used as an attractive counterpoint to the line art. Different textures are available on these tone sheets, and sometimes one like an ink spatter for a snowstorm effect can be used effectively.

2-66. Christmas cards are a good way to send greetings, because the message can be personalized as well. The french-fold on the 8½ × 11 inch format fits the baronial envelopes stocked by the printer.

With note cards for personal use it is assumed that they will be used one at a time, so they are not pre-folded or scored for folding. If one were to use a note card for a Christmas message, then it might be convenient to have the instant printer make one or both of the folds to save time. But if the quantity is only a hundred or so, it doesn't take too long to set up a table and run through the stack by hand, using a stick or burnisher to crease the fold. If the user does the handwork, the postage ends up being far the most expensive part of instant printing personal note cards.

2-67. These are the sizes of envelopes most often used for stationery, note cards, Christmas cards, and Christmas greeting letters. The number 10 size at the top handles stationery, the next half-sheet stationery, or stationery sheets that are folded in half before making the customary two folds. The squarish shape at the bottom is the baronial envelope that fits the quarter sheet size.

2-68. Portions of notepaper or note card art may be used effectively to decorate personalized envelopes near the return address.

ENVELOPES for use with personal notepaper and note cards are treated differently from business stationery. It is always convenient and more finished to have them printed with a return address and perhaps also decoration. The correct form for personal stationery places the return address on the back flap of the envelope without any decoration. But instant printing has an extra charge for the more difficult job of printing on the flap of a formed envelope.

A more informal approach is to take a portion of the decoration on the notepaper and place it on the front of the envelope with the return address. To achieve this, the decoration on the notepaper can be cut, repositioned, and used to do the paste-up for the envelope design. The notepaper design can also be reduced with a copier, if this is more appropriate for the smaller space of the envelope.

The name and address can be done with transfer type, with a typewriter, or by using printed material. Of course, use of transfer type or typesetting provides a wider and more interesting choice of type of design to go with the decorative motif. Some people are able to do legible and artistic lettering. The user's own handwriting can also serve, and an artistic effect is often achieved by using a pen different from the usual ball-point. Chisel and fountain pens will give a different appearance to hand-drawn letters. Calligraphy with a chisel-point pen is attractive, if practiced enough to have the necessary flow. Various methods combine for different effects. Transfer type initials may be used with the typewriter or with calligraphy, the name done in one style and the address in another. Typewriter line spacing can be changed when the material is positioned on the paste-up.

A copier reduction in the size of the type will change its effect. This size reduction is especially helpful in enhancing the effect of calligraphy. The size of the entire paste-up may also be reduced by up to one-half as the art is photographed for the instant printing plate.

In practice, the effect of the design may have to be placed on the envelope to be evaluated. But it is not always practical to paste up material for reproduction on the actual envelope. Rather, it is easier to place it on a heavy piece of paper or board, indicating the corner of the envelope so that the design can be positioned correctly.

The array of envelopes, their sizes, kinds, and papers, is confusing. It is easier and more convenient to work with and purchase from the instant printer's stock, which is specialized for printing requirements.

The standard number 10 envelope, measuring 9½ × 4 3/16

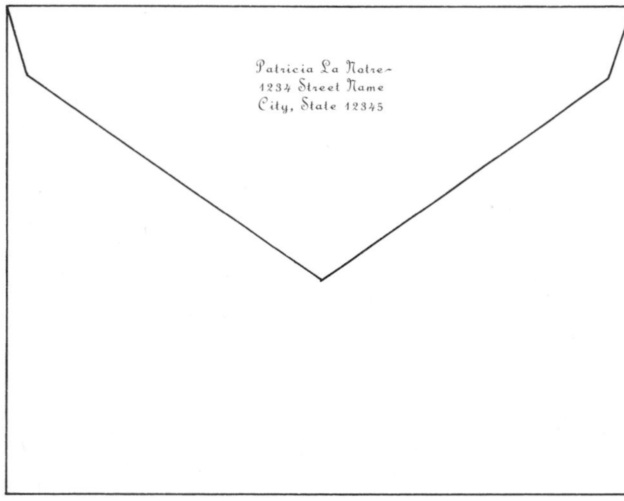

2-69. The return-address position for the return address on the formal envelope is on the flap, as shown here on the baronial size.

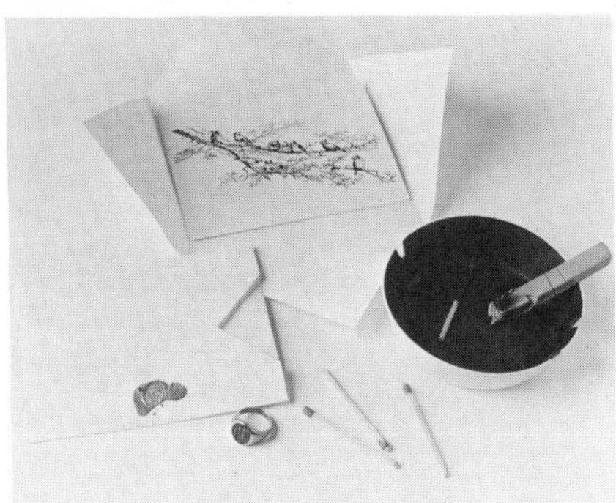

2-70. For a note card an envelope can be handmade with notepaper cut square and folded around the card.

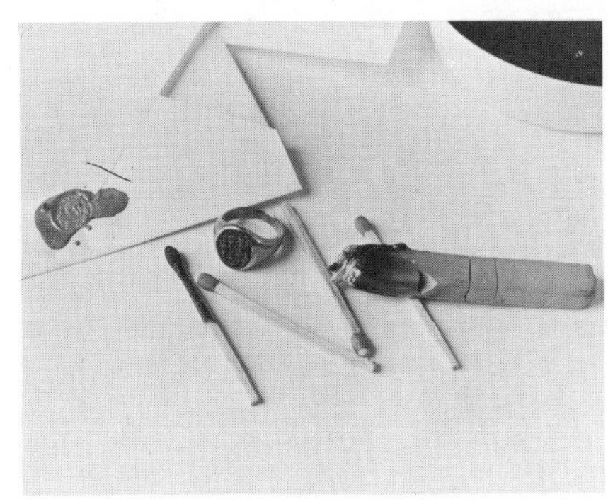

2-71. Colored sealing wax and a crest ring or signet stamp put the finishing touches on the handmade envelope.

inches, is fine for 8½ × 11 inch notepaper. When the 8½ × 11 inch sheet is cut or folded in half-size format, the notepaper can use a number 6 envelope, measuring 6 × 3 9/16 inches. Note cards done on one-half of the 8½ × 11 inch sheet fold down to fit a 5¾ × 4 7/16 inch envelope. This squarish shape is called baronial. If notecards are made smaller than the one-quarter sheet size, smaller baronial envelopes can be found at a stationery store, sized all the way down to gift-card size. When note cards are done in a smaller size, they will have to be planned to fit an available envelope, and very small sizes will prove difficult to print.

Envelopes that match stationery colors are stocked by some printers only in the standard number 10 size, with smaller sizes unavailable in colors. There is no rule that everything has to match, but if you prefer it, be sure to check on inventory. For this reason, it is sometimes a good idea to start with the envelope when designing stationery sets.

The printing of envelopes is usually done by the instant printer as a one-day service, because envelopes take a special press set up, which is not done till the end of the day.

Though not many people do this, a very satisfactory envelope can be handmade from a square piece of paper. An 8½ × 11 inch sheet is trimmed to 8½ × 8½ inches for this. The note card or square-folded letter is then placed on the square sheet, which is at a 45 degree diagonal. The right and left sides are folded in; then the bottom is folded up, and the top folded over it. This handmade envelope is then sealed with glue, a sticker, or sealing wax and a signet, as people did before the days of preformed envelopes. Paper for hand making envelopes can be prepared with instant printing. Art is designed to fall in the correct position on the sealed sheet, and the instant printing and cutting is handled as it would be for any other design. Small tick marks will help with aligning and folding the paper in the absence of a note card or folded notepaper to fold around.

Such designs as handmade envelopes are impressive, artistic, and fun to do, but it is undoubtedly easier to use a conventional envelope, printed with the return address. A repetition of the notepaper design on the envelope adds to the flavor.

BOOKPLATES create an identity for a private library. And for collectors who lend books, they provide a way to help the book find its way home.

The design of bookplates has a long tradition. The conventional one is on a rectangular sheet roughly 3 × 4 inches and includes an illustration or decorative motif. Often a phrase or thought is carried along with the owner's name. The phrase can be as simple as "From the library of . . . " or "This book belongs to . . . . " Some might use a family motto or perhaps some poetry. A practical example is a rhyme like, "Neither a lender or a borrower be, but if you are, see that this book returns to me."

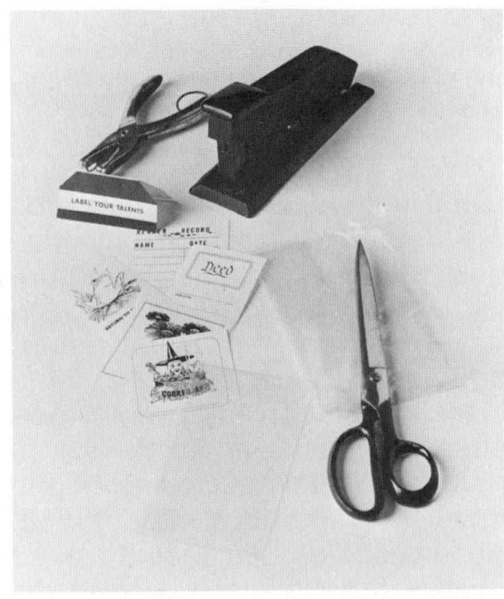

2-72. Bookplates packaged in a plastic bag make a nice gift. Besides bookplates other kinds of collections can use identity labels. For craft items: label your talents.

Bookplates also employ a great variety of decorative motifs. The design can be attuned to individual ideas, which suggests ordering a special illustration from an artist. Illustrations can be fanciful or funny, traditional or realistic, imaginative or surreal, or whatever is suggested by a collection's theme or by a collector's concept. Purely abstract decorative motifs can be used. Antiques are a rich source for more gen-

2-73. Bookplates invite many treatments and styles of art, Even though there is a tradition of bookplate design, novelty and personalized statement are appropriate.

eral themes and it is possible to adapt a theme suggested by the finding of some piece of antique art. Old sorts from printer's catalogs can suggest a design, and decorative chapter endings also offer ideas. Transfer art and clip art provide readily available decorative designs, and borders or specialized lettering can also be used to make up an individualized design.

The limited size of the bookplate may pose a problem when the intended piece of art is too large for the space. A copier that reduces will handle line art for a reduction, and if the art has sufficiently heavy lines, a reduction of the reduction. Otherwise a photostat may be used to reduce the art for a same-size paste-up. With sufficient planning the paste-up for the design can always be done for instant printing at double size, then reduced by 50 percent for the actual printing. Art that requires a halftone screen, like photographs and tonal illustrations, can always be reduced when the halftone screen is made. To accommodate the small size of a bookplate, type can be added to the picture area by using pressure-sensitive transfer type on top of the halftone photoprint.

Transfer type is available in some faces in opaque white as well as black. The white letters provide a surer reproduction when used on a screened print, though black can be used over the lighter-toned areas. Because a screened photoprint is made of small black and white dots, it is line art, and both ink lines and white paint can be used on and around the print to create a design for instant printing reproduction.

Bookplates are traditionally printed on a dry, gum-backed stock that is wetted to make it stick. It is dampened on the corners and tipped in, leaving most of the area free-floating, because too much moisture causes the paper to shrink and warp the sheet to which it is attached. When dry, the adhesive forms a permanent bond. A bookplate is usually placed on the front of the binding sheet at the beginning of a hardcover book. Soft-cover, perfect-bound books may pose a special problem, because they often have no binding sheet, so a new location must be found for the bookplate. The inside of the front cover is one solution. A very small bookplate for the outside of the front cover might also be a good idea for collectors like mystery fans, who lend books back and forth.

New adhesives also provide a durable bond for bookplates. They as well as labels can be printed on contact adhesive sheets. Once its backing is removed, the bookplate will adhere

2-75. Adhesive-backed stock can be used for bookplates and labels, though bookplates traditionally use dry gum stock and are only tipped in.

2-74. A number of different designs can be assembled for printing on one sheet. They are then cut apart at the broken line, which, of course, would not be on the finished paste-up.

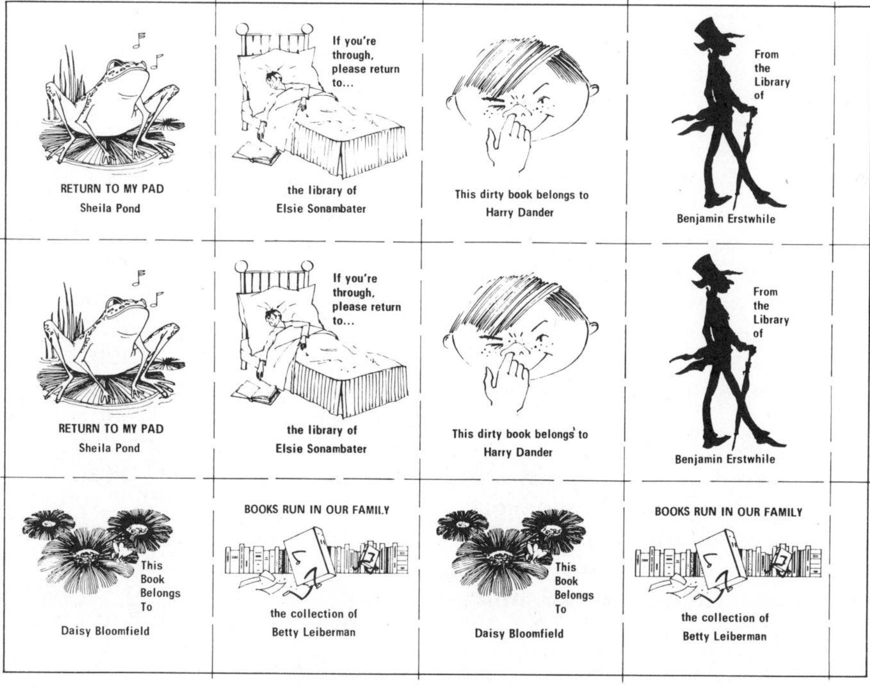

over the entire surface without warping. But when this ready-to-stick adhesive is placed on a fibrous sheet, it is difficult to remove without taking some of the sheet with it. The adhesive tack will release from a smooth surface, such as a varnished softcover, and the label can be peeled off again, though with time it will tend to stick permanently.

Since bookplates are small, copies are made of the design to fill the area on an 8½ × 11 inch sheet. This offers the possibility of different kinds of designs as well. There are many other things besides books that we collect and share with others. Publications, records, and tapes also form libraries and also call for special identifying designs. Children can use identity labels for floating items, school lunches, textbooks, and toys. Other variations might be ownership labels, signature labels, address labels, lost-and-found labels, and others. Each variation presents a special design problem. Records, album covers, and tape cassettes would call for labels in smaller sizes than the conventional bookplate. Though instant printing requires the rectangular shape for a label, small quantities can be trimmed with scissors, to a circular shape, for instance, that would fit a record.

The versatile contact adhesive will stick to almost any surface, and its use makes labels that will stick to plastic, metal, and glass as well as paper. This suggests even further uses for label designs: a maker's label for sculptures and other handmade objects.

Instant printed designs are conceived of in black and white, as this is the most economical, but colored ink can also be used. Small numbers of labels can be hand-colored with markers, if the design has an area suitable for this treatment. This provides color inexpensively, suggesting possible unique gift items.

Collectors will be happy to have a label to identify and preserve their treasures. The inclusion of the name distinguishes the design from commercial ones. And instant printing provides the means of obtaining what would once have been prohibitively expensive.

2-76. A special bookmark is welcome when included with a gift copy of a book. Personalized bookmarks are also a nice touch, and can be done in several ways.

BOOKMARKS are so much used as to need no description, yet even a slip of paper can be the object of a great variety of designing. The paper bookmarks most generally seen are advertisements, and bookstores put them in the package with every book sold. Far from such crass commercialism instant printed bookmarks may be whatever is wanted, full of the spirit of fun. They can be shaped to all sorts of interesting designs.

More than just elongated slips of paper, they can be shaped for note-taking or numbering. They can be cut at angles or cut with pinking-shears. They can be drilled for hanging, punched, colored, folded, and more. Tedious but effective, they can be notched with a flap that holds them in position. Perhaps even better, they can fold over and capture the page they are holding. Subject to all kinds of hand-finishing, the bookmark can have other pieces attached to it to make it more interesting.

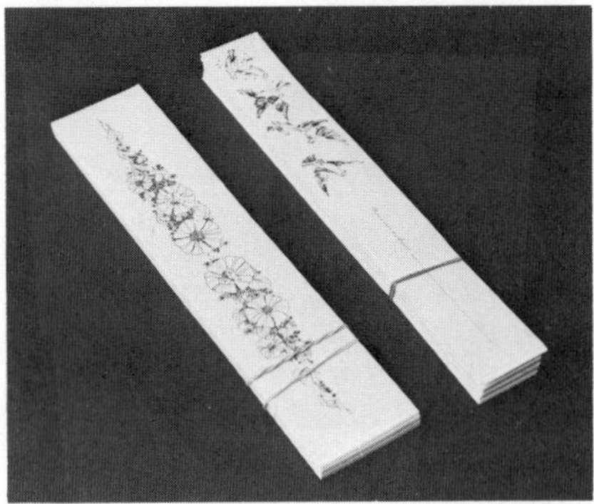

2-77. Each of these designs folds at the center, so that the bookmark stays in place.

We may think of a bookmark as a place saver when we're in the middle of an exciting story, but they have other functions. The researcher places bookmarks to locate ideas, the copyist to mark copy, the teacher to locate a subject, the poet to remember a phrase, and the music writer to find a melody.

The many personalized uses suggest all manner of graphic themes for the decoration of this bit of paper. For example, someone's elegant library might well need a monogrammed bookmark. Like bookplates, bookmarks help to complete a collection, and art derived from the bookplate might simply be reduced to fit new dimensions. Printer's sorts, for example, are useful for art treatment because of their small size. Depending on the use envisioned for the bookmark, various kinds of copy can be included in the design, purposeful as well as playful.

Bookmarks make fine gifts. It

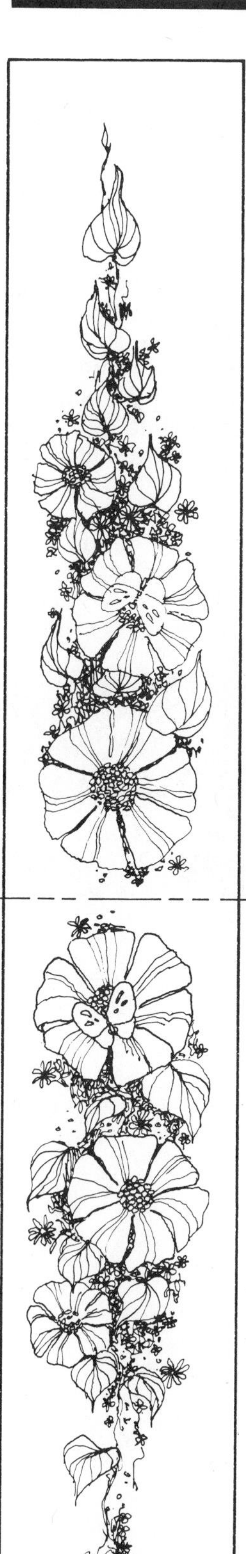

2-78. The design shown in the photograph. The dotted line indicating the fold would not necessarily be included in the art.

2-79. Bookmark designs can be personalized, like bookplates. This one has a notch cut near the top, indicated by the dotted line, where the bookmark would hold the page.

2-80. Hand finishing produces different effects. Pinking shears are used on the serrated edge at the top. The hole and angled cuts at the bottom are added also.

is a good idea to include a bookmark with a Christmas card and one should be tucked inside every gift book.

Printing can be done on one side only, or the other side can match. A number of designs can fit into one 8½ × 11 inch sheet. The 8½ inch depth should be enough for the length of the bookmark, and sometimes the width of the sheet runs with the grain of the paper, making the bookmark stiffer in its length. Bookmarks can be printed on any paper, but the heavier ones work best. Index board is to be preferred because of its weight.

These handy place savers are fun, but even fun takes some planning. It is better to spend a little time and produce one that will wear well during its long life. Perhaps the best idea for instant printing bookmarks is to fill with bookmark designs the areas on the sides of a sheet left over when printing some other project. For the piggyback ride with another instant printing job it is usually best if simple line art is used, not halftones, because this does not require special exposure to reproduce properly. Then, all that is needed is to trim the bookmark to the required shape, and sometimes even this follows with the cuts required to separate the other printing job.

Having the design ready when the opportunity presents itself for a "free ride" means that the bookmark becomes an attractive, functional use of what would otherwise have been scrap paper. It becomes that unusual thing: something for nothing.

2-81. Die-cut stickers are manufactured on stock with an adhesive finish and mounted on a backing from which they can easily be removed. The stock comes in colors as well as white.

STICKERS—essentially small labels—are a versatile item to be decorated with seals, crests, signets, emblems, ornaments, and symbols, depending on their use. They may be designed for fun, identification, decoration, information, or propaganda. New developments in adhesives bring new possibilities.

If designer labels are chic, then a sticker is one way to identify a number of handmade products. Stickers with logos could be designed for the artist, photographer, ceramicist, and hobbyist. Another use is that of distinctively designed seals for wrapping packages for birthdays and holidays. Have you ever seen anniversary stickers? Or a "Sorry, I'm late" sticker? There is always room for comment, and stickers can be made to advertise or direct attention to ideas. Causes may have stickers; to champion one, sticker it. Insignia of social groups and club emblems can be used, as may proverbs, funny animals, gold stars, and merit badges. A couple of specific applications might be; "Flowers arranged by . . . " for a vase, "Baked by . . . " for wrapping homemade bread. A crest, signet, or monogram serve as an identity label, for example, when applied to a person's possessions.

Art may be obtained from printer's sorts, clip art, and transfer type, or it can be done especially for the purpose. Stickers are a good place for one's own art: originality, styling, and distinctiveness determine success. A design for a monogram can be made by selecting transfer type initials and designing the placement of the letterforms. Some monograms fit a rectangular shape best; others work better in a circle. It depends on the way the design of the letters is worked out. Again, oversized line art can be reduced either by a copier or a photostat. Since a large number of copies is needed to fill the printing sheet, it is practical to reduce and copy art with instant printing. It can be reduced by precise amounts up to one-half its original size.

To make stickers with instant printing, both dry gum stock and contact adhesive stock may be used. The latter is generally preferred because of its ability to stick on virtually any relatively smooth surface. While dry gum stock can be cut into small sizes, the practical limit for the trimmer is probably about 1½ × 1½ inches minimum. Trimming the contact adhesive stock has to be limited to about 2 × 2 inches minimum, because smaller pieces

2-82. The die-cut shapes come in many sizes, but if they are too small, the problem of getting them in register increases.

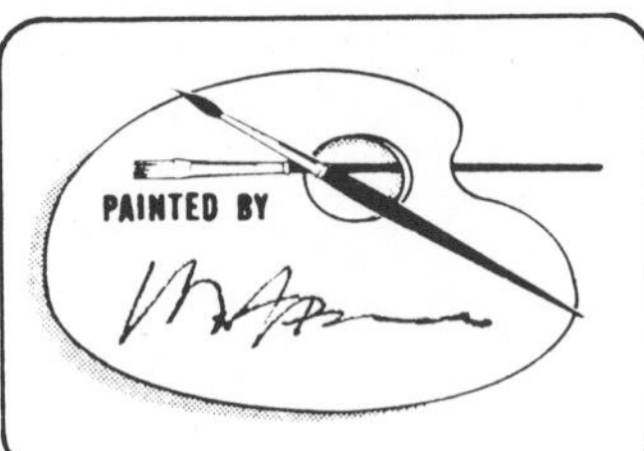

TOP SECRET

2-83. Labels invite all kinds of designs and uses, even commentary.

will fall between cracks on the backing, making them difficult to peel.

The shape should be held to a 90 degree rectangle. For a small quantity the handwork of trimming could be undertaken. Smaller stickers should use prepared sheets that have die-cut labels attached to a backing. These are available in some variety from most instant printers and in still greater variety from stationery stores. They are sold in differently sized pre-cut rectangles with rounded corners or circles of various measures. Some are also to be had in color—yellow, red, blue, and a few also in silver and gold. The label sheets should be seen before the preparation of the art, so that the design can be related to the exact size and shape of the label.

Since the sheets are mechanically accurate, they can be pulled through the press in register for each label blank. It would be wise, however, to keep the design away from the edges of the label to allow for some slight shift of position during printing. This also applies to any kind of design that echos the edge of the label, something that would make obvious any slight shifting of position to the detriment of the result. These tactics minimize the problem of accurate registry. The smaller the design, the greater the need for accuracy in sizing and placing it. Extremely small stickers will prove most difficult because of the greater need for close printing registry.

It is very important in making up the printing sheet that each copy of the design be positioned truly. An accurate drawing of the label sheet can be made on a piece of paper, but a better way is to use a light table with the paper taped over the label sheet. The paste-up for printing is then positioned exactly where the label is. Another method is to use a sheet of heavy tracing paper over the label sheet. But probably the best and simplest way is to use the white label-sheet itself as a mounting base for placing the designs. This is only possible, however, if the labels are white and the label backing sheet is a light, non-reproducing color ; blue is preferred.

Printing a small number of label sheets yields a large number of stickers; twenty-five sheets with forty labels each produces a thousand stickers. For this reason, it is practical to do several designs. Place those with the most critical register at the head of the sheet, since the gripper will feed this part first, and it has the least variation of position.

Seals for exterior use or those that are subject to moisture, like window stickers, can be painted with plain or acrylic varnish to keep moisture out. A little pigment added to the varnish tints white sheets of labels.

The paper will not stand up to repeated flexing, preventing its use on fabric. For stickers on clothes, use the 8½ × 11 inch sticker sheet on a copier, transferring designs to an iron-on transfer sheet. By doing this on a color copier, the design can be made in any primary color as well as black. The transfer sheet is then cut apart and ironed onto the fabric.

In all their variety stickers offer a real challenge to the designer, and because of their ubiquity they need to be well designed. Clever ideas are fun, but it is no easy task to come up with a winning design. Not everyone can create a CBS "eye" or a Chiquita banana logo.

2-84. Chiquita® banana started a sticker fad. This is not exactly a banana, but it is a good, subject to endorse for quality.

2-85. Decorate your mail with your own stamp designs, if you like, but be sure to include the proper amount of genuine postage.

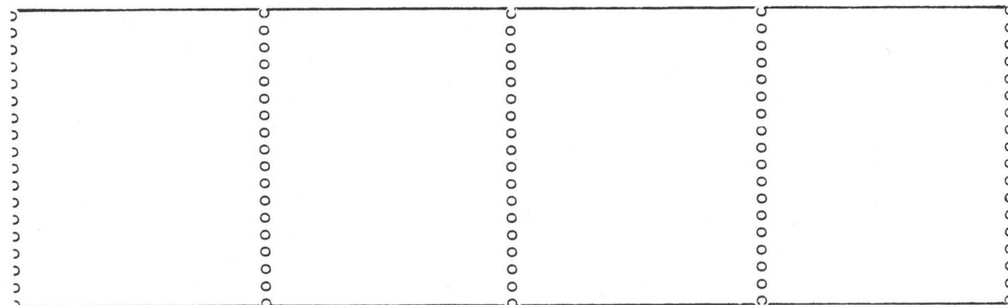

2-86. Because stamps are so tiny, they are hard to work on at their actual size. These borders are one-third oversize, but a 75 percent copier reduction will take them down to size. This is an often seen format size, but there are a number of others.

STAMPS tickle the philatelist's fancy. Like posters and prints, philately is an artform for collectors, who often dream of making their own designs for pure fun. Now with instant printing they will be able to.

The history of stamp usage shows that in addition to mail and taxes, they are also used for games and prizes, for gifts and charities, for trade, rationing, and licenses. Handsome government issues of postage stamps commemorate, celebrate, and memorialize, generally putting forth the concerns of national ideology. This gives the hobbyist-designer a wide area, in which to develop designs. His imagination can range from designing postage for an imaginary nation to commemorating fanciful events, from celebrating eccentricities to glorifying nonsense. More practical topics are charities, causes, and memorabilia that can travel on envelopes along with genuine, canceled U.S. postage. The small printed label is able to comment from a ringside position. As decorations stamps have a close kinship with stickers in all their possibilities.

The design of a stamp might be likened loosely to that of a miniature poster. Each uses words and pictures, and in each the design must be simple for the best effect. Donald Evans, well-known fine artist, made his miniature watercolors of nations he invented into editions of stamps that have been shown in museums around the country.

Government postage stamps come in more than one size, but for realism the stamp hobbyist might closely approximate the small size of conventional issue. Stamps are sized to the printer's measure of picas. Six picas equal one inch, and measuring is done with a pica scale. The size of the conventional U.S. postage stamp is 5 × 6 picas, customarily seen in a vertical format.

The typical perforations on a sheet of stamps might be overlooked. Instead and less expensively the perforations between stamps and on the edges can be simulated. A sheet of stamps is placed face down on black paper; then the black dots are reproduced on a copier. Still more realistically, typesetting can produce a row of properly sized and spaced dots by using the letter "o." A printer's dotted leader, dash leader, or dotted rule also approximate the divisions between stamps.

Art for stamp designs is found in printer's sorts, suitably small to fit the tiny face of the stamp. Some clip art books also provide reductions of art that can be used. The letters of course may be produced with transfer type, since few letters are involved.

2-87. The reduction in size is easy to plan with a diagonal line. As long as the corner of the enlarged rectangle is on the diagonal line, the art will have the right proportions when it is reduced.

2-88. Small art, like the printer's sort at the left or the clip art at the right, can be used to make stamp designs.

Because stamps are so small, it is much better to do the art and design at a proportionately larger size and then to reduce it for reproduction. Line art can be conveniently and inexpensively reduced to 75 or 60 percent of its original size on a copier called a duplicator. When using a copier, the design must be planned at exactly 1⅓ of its size to reduce by 75 percent, or to 1⅔ of its size to reduce by 60 percent. If the reduction is done when making the plate for instant printing, the art can be exactly twice its reproduction size. Use of a photostat would permit the art to be up to five times its size.

Actual stamp art has extremely fine lines, and this engraving quality can be imitated by using art with the same line technique used for engravings.

Individual stamp designs are made up in rows for instant printing. Several individual designs might be done, then reduced and copied with instant printing, so as to have a sufficient number to fill a sheet.

Realism is enhanced by printing on dry gum stock exactly the way regular stamps are done. They can be trimmed by pushing the sheet from the far end and trimming the rows of stamps into 1 inch strips, down to a minimum end piece of about 1½ inches. The individual stamps are then cut by hand from the strip.

The effort to simulate realism should not be misconstrued to mean attempting to duplicate, copy, or photograph actual government issue, because this would be forgery, subject to fines and imprisonment. The suggestion is a play upon realism for the amusement of the hobbyist.

Another way of producing stamps is to follow the method used for making stickers, when the blank sheet of labels is used for printing. This provides conveniently separated stamps and looks very finished, though it does not have the same degree of realism. Printed designs can be hand tinted in small quantities or actually done in color by using a color copier. Such a copier does the line art in a primary color by blocking the other two, and it can also be used to duplicate a hand-colored sheet.

The instant-printed stamps the philatelist has designed can be the start of an entirely new collection to treasure or to trade.

2-89. Art for individual stamps can be done in rows to simulate a roll of stamps.

2-90. The row of stamp designs is made into art for a printing sheet with copies of the original design. If you use a copier, use the same original because copiers do not hold the size exactly. The copies can be placed top to bottom, like the first three rows, or done in separate rows to fill the sheet and simulate strips from a roll of stamps. The separate strips could be trimmed by machine, but the others are probably too close. Naturally, the black line at the top and bottom of the design is not necessary.

2-91. Phone pads are good to have, and this is probably the most frequent application of design.

PHONE PADS are necessities for doodling and even for taking down phone numbers, but they may be made special, when they are designed with art. Like notepaper, the sheets can be decorated and then padded into books with instant printing.

These pads should be designed for a purpose. For example, matched sizes make these sheets suitable for filing, and with drilling they can also be inserted into a ring-binder phone book. Padding holds the sheets for convenient use.

Decoration for phone pads may be anything from doodle starters to organizers for files. A design might be personalized with name or monogram. Little pictures add a light touch. Alligators gobble up information; hippopotamuses get fat on it; elephants always remember; and giraffes plan ahead.

The colors of the sheets might vary, with a series of colors collated for binding into pads. In the above example, each animal could have a different color. Padding is a form of binding with the added convenience that the top sheet comes off easily and the next page is a pleasant surface to work on.

Everyone needs an assortment of other kinds of pads. We use little slips of paper for shopping lists, errand lists, idea memos, our schedules, accounting, family messages, and so on. These can also be designed with art and personalized. None of these scribblings is to be kept forever, but they have in common the characteristic of being important until they are used. The relationship of lists and jottings to organization and the passage of time suggests time and season as themes for graphic design. A snowflake for winter or calendar events, like the Fourth of July.

Larger sheets for diary writing may be made into pads and at the same time be drilled for a ring binder. (Permanent bindings have a way of preserving mistakes.) Workbooks could also be treated this way, and those pages worth saving would find their way into a binder storage.

For small phone pads, the 8½ × 11 inch instant printing sheet may be filled with a number of different designs. There is also nothing to prevent using the more durable index board for permanent information. Normal 20-pound bond paper pads down to a little less than ½ inch thickness for a hundred sheets. Index board would pad more thickly so that fifty-sheet pads might be preferable.

The sheet, made up with different designs, is planned for trimming and padding, and the various design elements are assembled and mounted in place as a paste-up. Pads can be made in any size from the 8½ × 11 inch sheet, though a small one is desirable for phone use. One practical format allows the sheet to be cut into eights yielding a pad of 2¾ × 4½ inches. The padding is usually done after printing and cutting, and this makes for a one-day order to allow drying time for ink and glue.

Who remembers a phone number the first time they hear it, unless they write it down? Who resists doodling as they talk on the phone? Individually designed phone pads add character to the clutter that accumulates beside a phone. They may even help to organize it.

2-92. Designs for phone pads can be useful or decorative and use papers of different colors.

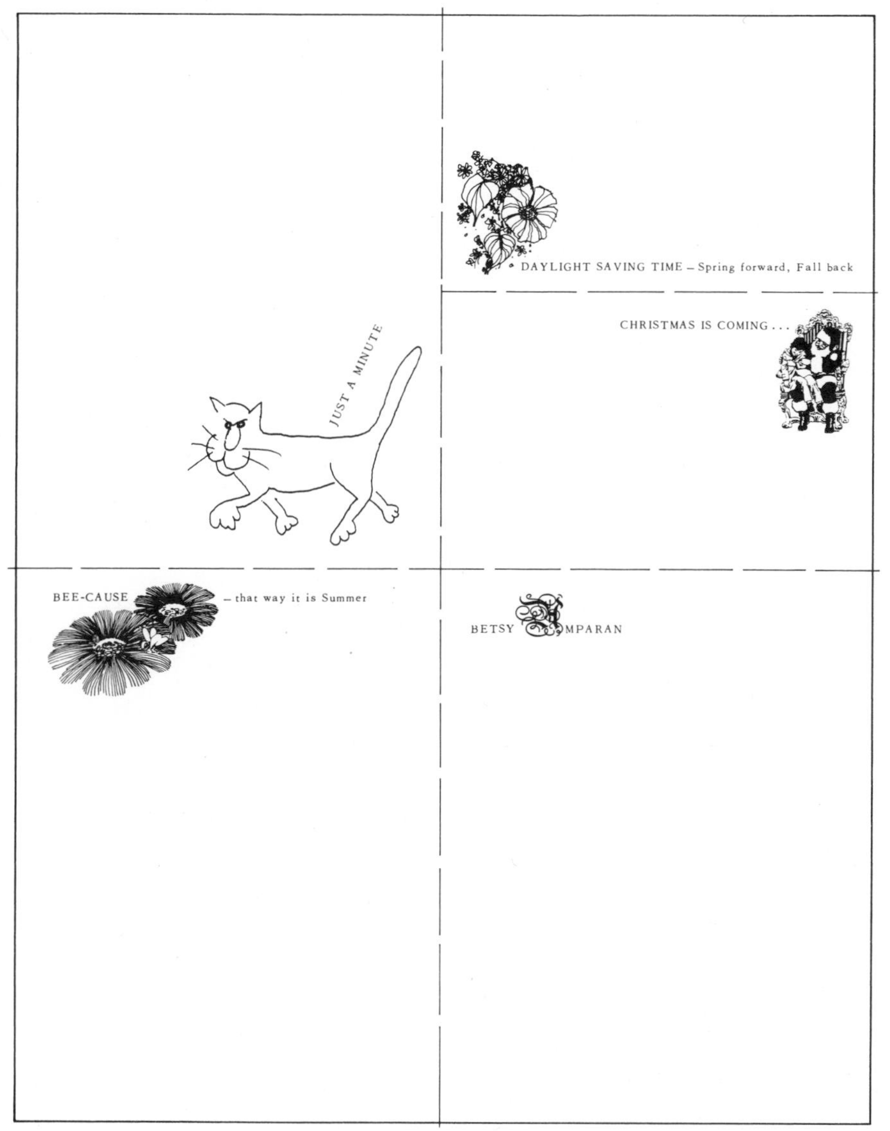

2-93. The designs are positioned in a way that works. Two convenient sizes are shown here.

2-94. A small plastic bag of gift tags makes a welcome party gift.

TAGS are tied on gifts, but they also have special uses for hobbyists and others. Makers of garments or dolls, knitting or crocheting can use tags to identify and explain. Special price tags are made for bazaars or garage sales.

A conventional gift tag is a square when folded. The front cover is the place for design and comment; the inside is for writing names and sentiment. They are like miniature greeting cards. Another style of gift tag design doesn't fold, presenting just one surface. There is space within the design itself for names, or the back is used for writing. Probably the greatest use for gift tags is during the Christmas and Chanukah holiday season when boxes

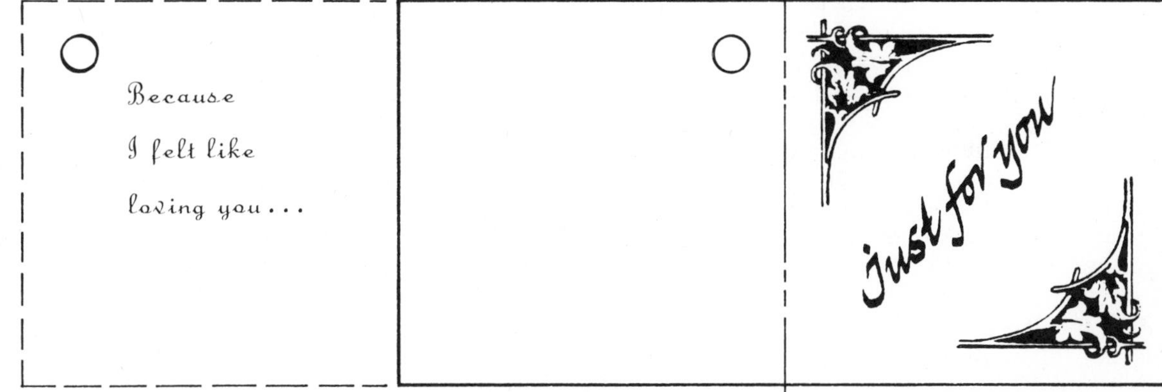

2-95. A gift tag can be done in single, double, or triple panels, each producing a different kind of design. Punching a hole for ribbon or yarn tie and folding can be done by hand for a small quantity.

must be identified, but other occasions call for sentiment and gifts, too.

Though gift tags can be stuck with seals, they are most often tied to the wrapping of a present. Tying the tag means the addition of a hole and a piece of yarn. This involves handwork.

For the graphic art, clip art and transfer type offer a variety of border designs and cartouches, and small art from sorts can also be added. Holiday themes are plentiful. Comments and thoughts are part of the graphic design, reflecting the reason for the gift. A simple "to" and "from" or "a gift for you" might be enough. "Just because I felt like it" and "thinking of you" are other ideas. All the different holidays suggest varied art motifs and copy to be treated in unique and personalized ways.

Index board is suitable for gift tags, but because they are small, a heavy paper will also do very well. This is the place to use colors, even bright ones, mixed to provide variety. Yarn strings add to the color possibilities.

Since the grain usually runs the length of the paper, printing the tags horizontally on the page means that they will fold with the grain. Paper grain is a factor when folding a small tag of heavy paper. For short grain, a typical layout for gift tags on the 8½ × 11 inch instant-printing sheet would have two rows of four tags that fold down to 2⅛ inches square. There is no space for press grippers to fall within such a small design, so the designs are mounted for printing with at least ½ inch at the end. If there is waste space there is an opportunity for a bookmark to be printed with the tag designs. Printing on paper with a long grain makes space for two more tags. With eight or ten tags to the sheet, a small printing rapidly produces a large number of tags. Making more tags than needed provides

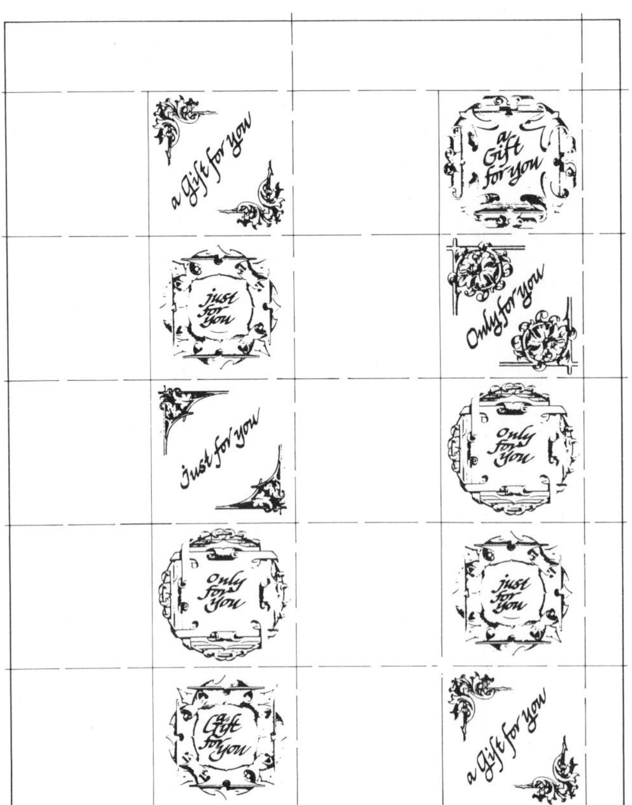

2-96. This layout for gift tags is for paper with vertical grain. The small size of the item makes the grain a more important factor in folding.

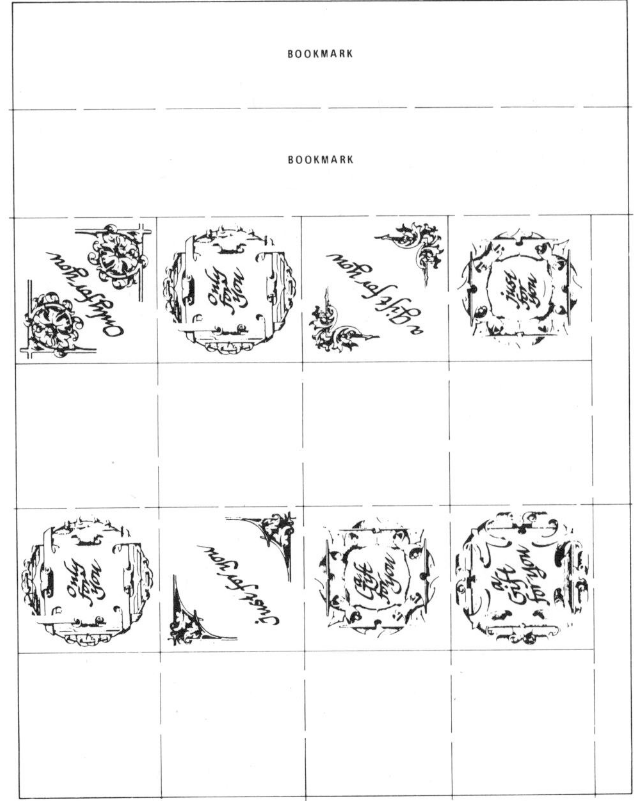

2-97. This layout of tag designs is for paper with horizontal grain. There are two fewer tags in the layout, but there is space at the end to make a three panel design. If not, use the excess paper for bookmark designs that also need index board or stiff paper.

a clever bridge gift or party prize.

It is assumed that for personal use the work of folding and making up the tags will be done by the user. The tags can be trimmed to size by the instant printer, and they can also be drilled, but punching a hole doesn't add much to the work of the user. A ledger punch provides a larger hole than does the usual paper punch, and this allows for the use of ribbon instead of yarn. With the larger punch, the tie might be left off in favor of using the package ribbon to hold the gift tag.

It is important to match the size and design of the tag to its purpose. If tags are being made for little, handcrafted dolls they would be smaller than gift tags, and the copy would read: "Originals by . . . . " If the craftsman wants to include an explanation on the tag, one simple method is to use the typewriter and then to get a reduction from a copier.

Since the printing is only on one side, a design could be printed on what will be the front and back of a folded tag. Then when front and back are glued together, it becomes a two-sided card. A variation of this treatment is to make two folds with three panels, gluing the cover panel down on the center section. Printing on one side will thus do the cover and both halves inside the fold.

As well as being tied to the item, a tag can fold over and catch part of it. This permits the use of staples to both mount and hold the cover down.

Instant printing invites the hobbyist to create inexpensive tags for craft items, and sometimes an original statement on a tag explains the product. All that's really required is a clever idea and the art.

2-98. Tickets, passes, and claim checks are often useful for various social events. Instant printing provides a way to do a small number.

TICKETS with a professional look for non-commercial social events can be made in small quantities with instant printing. Whether it be a costume ball, bazaar, charity raffle, amateur theater, or whatever, tickets to help organize the activity can be produced inexpensively.

Their design must fit the requirements of distributing, accounting, and handling. A variety of techniques can be devised to make up the art for them. The design is of necessity primarily composed of copy, although small pieces of decorative art can be used, too. The subject sets the theme for the design.

Within the practicalities of printing and handling, the necessary information on it will determine the size of the ticket. We normally see a range in sizes used for them from the small tab used in mechanized ticket dispensers at the movies to the larger boards used for reserved seating in theaters.

The need for numbering and perforating must be decided first because of the effect on the ticket's design. Areas for numbers, duplication of information on the stub, and space for perforation become graphic requirements. With smaller quantities of tickets it is possible to number them by hand. Larger quantities will have to be numbered by the instant printer at additional cost. The need for stubs raises the question of whether the ticket should be perforated, again adding to the cost of printing.

The focus of the graphics is usually the title of the event. Other pertinent information: date, time, location, cost, sponsor, and whatever else is necessary. Few of us have occasion really to look at the design of a ticket or at the information on it, but to be functional a ticket must have the necessary contractual information. Beyond the title, most of the information on a ticket is small in size, so that the contractual information is sometimes minuscule. The operative information—ticket number or seating space—needs to be sized so as to be easy to find and read.

Since the graphics of a ticket

2-99. This ticket is numbered and perforated to provide a stub for record keeping. The dotted line indicates the perforation.

consist mainly of typography, it is helpful to use typesetting, with pictures or decoration handled as simple line-art. It is possible to use a photograph and to place type over it, though this involves the additional expense of photography and a halftone print. When using a photo, the art for instant printing is prepared most easily by double printing the type onto the halftone, so that the art is complete and ready to shoot.

Transfer type can be placed directly on a halftone, but another, more exacting way is to use a sheet of acetate to hold the transfer type. The clear acetate is placed in position over the entire paste-up, including the halftone, to make the instant-printing plate. With this method, though, the work must be kept meticulously clean, so that the acetate does not shadow the line-art underneath, causing unwanted images to expose and develop on the instant-printing plate. A positive film image may also be used over the art, overprinting text into a halftone.

Strike-on typesetting is very useful for an instant-printed ticket. It is usually less expensive than regular typesetting, done with metal or photocomposition.

For the lowest cost, it is possible to get the effect of typesetting with a typewriter. To make typewritten copy fit the confined space, it is reduced with a copier. The design is planned to use both full-size and reduced-size typing. The kind of typewriter that has interchangeable type faces provides additional choices for design when two fonts are mixed and used at different sizes. The sizing and composing of typewriter fonts in combination with transfer type gives the effect of typesetting. Actual typesetting can be sized to the design, but typewritten copy with copier reductions is harder to plan for size. There may have to be a little juggling on the paste-up to make everything fit. In such a small space the critical fitting might require some elasticity on the boundaries of the ticket to make the spacing look well.

A convenient size for a ticket done with instant printing would be 5¼ × 2⅛ inches. This size can be laid out in two rows of four with ½ inch left at the top for the press gripper. When requirements are more flexible, an 8½ × 14 inch sheet may be used, or the tickets made wider. Waste at the side can always be utilized with a bookmark design.

Placing tickets the length of the sheet makes a horizontal grain run across the ticket. If it is important to be able to tear off a ticket stub, and there is no perforation, it is easier to tear with the grain than across it. If perforation and numbering are done on the printed ticket, it should be large enough to handle easily and to feed on the press, no smaller than a business card.

Index board is good because of its stiffness. Colors enhance the ticket design as well as identity and coding.

Instant-printed tickets can be produced most economically when done simply with no numbering or perforation and with only the typewriter, rather than typesetting. Though the use of typesetting, art, photography, numbering, and perforation costs more, they do give an attractive, professional result.

Sometimes other printed items are needed for the same social event. A program might incorporate a design similar to that of the ticket and employ the same color and art motif. The identifying look that will result from this graphic treatment lends style to the whole event.

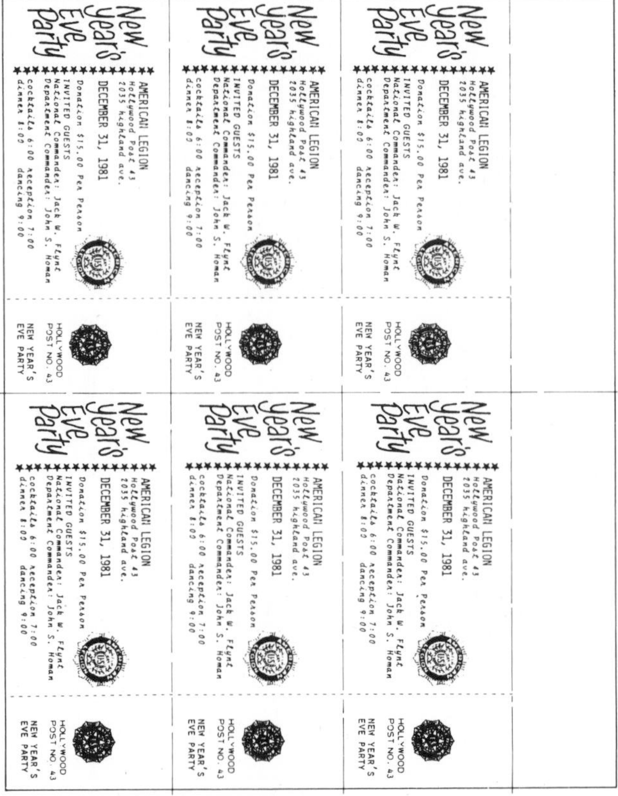

2-100. The design can be copied and laid out for printing this way, if it is not numbered and perforated. Perforation and numbering, which would be handled by the printer, call for printing fewer copies at one time, so that the perforation and numbering can be positioned. The dotted line runs in the direction of the paper grain, and the stub can be torn off along the line after bending.

APPLICATIONS 3

The increasing use of instant printing has brought with it a greater sophistication of products in their design and execution. As the industry of instant printing has developed, so has the range of services it offers and so has the range of products that users produce and apply to their own purposes.

If users start out by merely substituting instant printing for improved mimeographing, they soon learn how flexible the process is; then they learn how to adapt and apply it to produce products of their own design for their own needs. With repeated use, the application of the product to the need and purpose improves, the product idea and design improves, and the art technique and preparation improves.

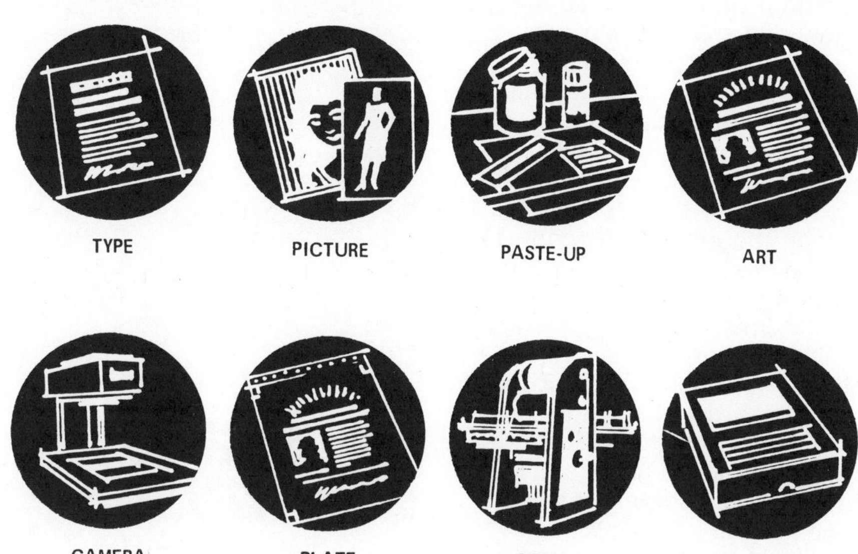

3-1. Learning the steps that produce graphic products becomes easier with experience, and knowledgeable users develop effective products.

The applicationof an instant-printing product is fundamental to its success. Business considerations of timeliness and value enter into this evaluation of purpose to which the product is applied. The idea for the product is necessarily guided by the purpose, and this in turn helps to develop the design. How well the product is thought out and designed contributes to the clarity of the communication. The art techniques and aesthetic sense used in preparing the art for the product help provide the quality that fulfills the design idea and serves the purpose of the application for an instant-printing product.

If it's true that we are Yankee traders by instinct, with a purpose for the application of instant-printing products, we can benefit from some help in formulating specific designs to serve our applications. In turn, if it is true that some people have a natural tendency to the temperament, dexterity, and aesthetic sense for executing instant-printing art, most anyone can learn to do finished pieces for products that will have the sophistication of a professional look.

There are few commercial artists, graphic designers, and business people after this period of development in the use of instant-printing art who have not made use of instant printing. Because of these developed skills applied to the instant-printing product, there are good examples of products to be found in most every instant-printing establishment. These products will be good examples of application, design idea, and art technique for producing the product.

More than the art for instant printing, application involves a number of considerations that go into and lead up to preparing the art for instant printing. The validity of all these considerations is proven by the success of the instant-printing product. To help users of instant printing develop their own ideas for the application to instant-printing art these tips follow proven methods for producing effective products.

GETTING YOUR OWN IDEAS TOGETHER

Instant printing has so many applications that most of us will make use of it at some time or another to support our activities. Through it we contact, invite, inform, announce, offer, sell, and otherwise communicate. To make proper use of it, we need to organize our thoughts sufficiently to put what we have to say into the form of a graphic product.

This process of organization is helped along by the formats that instant printing offers. These have standard uses, forms, and sizes. According to our needs, we then utilize the services of instant printing to create the product we have in mind. It is possible to use the formats that have been used before, though in ways that suit our own special needs. This does not mean that products cannot be invented; it simply means that it is easier to use existing formats than to create them from scratch. Organization then becomes a matter of adapting our ideas and information to the product format. What needs to be communicated can now be seen in relation to the product.

Any of the preceding examples of products may be used as models for different projects with similar purposes. The product that most nearly fits our purposes is the one selected as a guide.

With this approach gathering a series of similar products at the outset will provide further examples of design and technique. The best examples should be selected, of course, because they provide the most help. While looking at these examples for format, one studies how they can be adapted and improved. The more innovations brought to the format, the better. Eventually, this leads to designing one's own communications product from the ground up without a guide.

3-2. A bulletin board provides one way to communicate. The flier at lower left uses the clever heading: "I do windows, yes."

Three principles of communication suggest a guide for thinking and evaluation. No guide is all-inclusive, but these principles are tried and true. They sound simple but they are hard to follow.

First, the most effective communication focuses on no more than one primary point. The temptation for the user is to say too much, but decisions about what has to be said must lead to reconciling all the information with the main point.

Second, when other information has to be included, all of it should be subordinated to the main point. It is possible to follow the main point with a number of supporting details that are essential to the reader, but they should never conflict or compete with the chief idea. It is best if these follow-up points come in a sequence that is adapted to the needs of the reader. They should answer his questions in a logical sequence.

Third, these follow-up points should also lead the reader to a knowledge of how to pursue or react to the main idea. The information must be sufficient to provide a channel of action. For example, if a service is offered to the reader, a channel of information should be provided, so that the reader can obtain the service.

When in doubt about how much to include, simplify. The clearest, strongest communication is always the simplest. Additional bits of information that don't help the reader should be left out, so as not to blur the main idea. Most of us grasp one idea at a time, and after it has been grasped, it is much easier to assimilate a further thought that is based on it.

The last thing said is nearly as important as the first. The positions of first and last are one and two in rank of importance in communicating. As a rule, what is communicated cannot achieve the simplicity of the ideal, but an effective appeal that simply an-

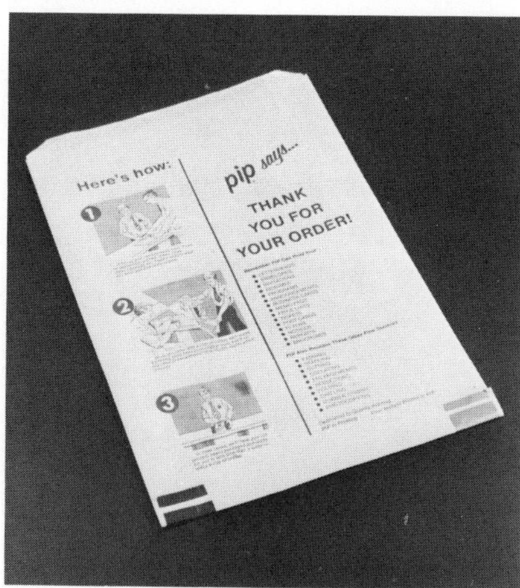

3-3. PIP© (Postal Instant Press) packages orders in a bag that promotes the products and services offered. The three illustrations explain the procedure and how the printer helps the user arrive at a product.

Remember PIP Can Print Your
- LETTERHEADS
- ENVELOPES
- INVITATIONS
- RESUMES
- PROGRAMS
- ANNOUNCEMENTS
- BUSINESS CARDS
- MEMO PADS
- PRICE LISTS
- TICKETS
- POST CARDS
- FLYERS
- NOTICES
- REPORTS
- BROCHURES

PIP Also Provides These Services
- PADDING
- STAPLING
- CUTTING
- COLLATING
- ENLARGEMENTS
- REDUCTIONS
- FOLDING
- DRILLING
- RUBBER STAMPS
- PHOTOCOPYING

3-4. These are the products and services listed by PIP© promotion.

swers the reader's first few questions and provides a path for action has the best chance of being understood and acted upon. Such a model for information, along with the example of a product that fits the purpose, should enable a user of instant printing to organize individual graphic communication.

COPYRIGHTS AND PLAGIARISM

Specific materials and presentation can be copyrighted, but a generic idea cannot. Using the work of someone else as a model means applying the format idea, not the specific art.

Copyright protects the ownership rights of written and graphic material; it is displayed as © or spelled out as COPYRIGHT with the date added. Registered names and trademarks are also protected by international agreement and law. A registered name is followed by ®. A protected trademark is followed by the small letters TM. Names and trademarks are generally capitalized. As an example, the specific name of Zipatone ® for the original halftone sheet is registered, but other manufacturers have picked up on the idea and make halftone sheets under other names. The *Mona Lisa* could be copyrighted, but that would not bar other portraits of smiling women.

Another area of legal restriction applies to instant printing and concerns the copying of government documents. While government publications are copyright-free, it is against the law to reprint any of them, and the instant printer will tell you of this as well as of the copyright laws. Besides, copying that dollar bill will quickly get all the wrong people interested in your work, Treasury Agents and the like.

The copyright law is intended to protect the originator's right to control their work and to gain remuneration from it. In the law's complexity there are many gray areas, like the custom of "fair use," where an attributed quotation can be made for critical use or study. Problems have grown with the copier and with the ease that instant printing can be used to duplicate printed pieces. With the new technology a question of private use has arisen, and after many years, it has yet to be definitively decided.

Letraset *instant lettering* ©

©LETRASET INTERNATIONAL LTD. 1972

© Zipatone Inc., Hillside, Ill. 60162 1974

FORMATT*

***Trademark**

Copyright 1981 by the Graphic Products Corporation, Rolling Meadows, IL 60008, U.S.A.

©VOLK

Copyright 1977 by Volk Corp., Pleasantville, N.J. The art contained herein is original and exclusive with Volk Corporation and resyndication — in whole or in part — for multiple resale in the form of stock engravings, stock mats, stock printing, etc. will be prosecuted.

3-5. © and ® indicate copyright and trademark registration. These examples of transfer type and clip art manufacturers show how they are used. The explanation in small type is usually located elsewhere on the page or in the publication. The clip art at the bottom has the copyright indication at the lower left corner, a © with the abbreviated corporation name.

Plagiarism is the theft and passing off as one's own the writings, art, words, and ideas of others. Therefore, using someone else's work as a model or guide requires the originator of an instant-printing piece to do individual work and to make specific application. In truth, while we can learn by imitation, we must also be free. Plagiarism reverses a constructive process of observation and learning into one of confinement and limitation. Too much copying inhibits the thinking of new ideas, better suited to individual needs.

The primary identification of a product format is its function and how it does what it does. The generic format of a product, such as a flier for example, is not subject to copyright. Instant printing offers a standard 8½ × 11 inch-size format, which can be used for a flier. Yet the way this instant-printing format is used is wide open to invention and design. The concepts about the formats of products are convenient, and instant-printing formats even more so. There is, however, no law that these formats must be observed or that new occasions will not cause the development of completely new graphic products. A product format can be revised and a completely new product be designed to make new use of the standard-size format system of instant printing. Further, it is always possible to revise, adapt, or even merge two product formats to form a new idea that will have a successful application.

In addition to the fundamental method of producing material with typesetting and original art, sources of material for use with instant printing are growing with the popularity of the process. Transfer type, transfer art, clip art, antique art, stock photos, and sorts are all available. These are produced by a growing number of suppliers and with improving quality. Sophisticated users of instant printing are also taking advantage of other ready art that can be photographed with an instant camera or taken from original design drawings.

Page 3

Certificate

Registration of a Claim to Copyright
in a published book manufactured in
the United States of America

FORM A

REGISTRATION NO. A 78836 DO NOT WRITE HERE

CLASS A

This Is To Certify that the statements set forth on this certificate have been made a part of the records of the Copyright Office. In witness whereof the seal of the Copyright Office is hereto affixed.

Register of Copyrights
United States of America

1. Copyright Claimant(s) and Address(es):

Name ....

Address ....

Name ....

Address ....

2. Title: .... (Title of book)

3. Authors:

Name .... (Legal name followed by pseudonym if latter appears on copies) Citizenship .... (Name of country)

Domiciled in U.S.A. Yes .... No .... Address ....

Name .... (Legal name followed by pseudonym if latter appears on copies) Citizenship .... (Name of country)

Domiciled in U.S.A. Yes .... No .... Address ....

Name .... (Legal name followed by pseudonym if latter appears on copies) Citizenship .... (Name of country)

Domiciled in U.S.A. Yes .... No .... Address ....

4. Date of Publication of This Edition:

.... (Month) (Day) (Year)

5. New Matter in This Version:

6. Book in English Previously Manufactured and Published Abroad: If all or a substantial part of the text of this edition was previously manufactured and published abroad in the English language, complete the following spaces:

Date of first publication of foreign edition .... (Year)

Was registration for the foreign edition made in the U.S. Copyright Office? Yes .... No ....

If your answer is "Yes," give registration number ....

EXAMINER

Complete all applicable spaces on next page

3-6. A copyright form is obtained from the copyright office. After it is filled in and returned to the copyright office with the fee, it is given a number, signed, stamped, and registered. This form would apply to a publication.

The copier is very useful to duplicate documents and a tremendous work saver for making copies for records and for private use. Instant printing, because it is used to produce greater quantities of work than a copier, is used to create original pieces in small print runs for distribution.

The great majority of instant printing is done without copyright, while published work with a larger investment is usualy copyrighted to protect the rights of the originators. A copyright can be obtained for any printed piece and for art by writing the Copyright Office, The Library of Congress, Washington, D.C. 20559 and asking for a form for that category of work. Upon registration, payment of a fee, and copyright notification on the published work, the copyright is in force.

Clip art is often copyrighted to prevent its use without authorization or payment. The same thing applies to stock photos with their attendant fees. Use of transfer materials and other prepared art is authorized by payment for their purchase.

Advertising, since additional circulation suits its purpose, is often not copyrighted. Yet it would not be a good idea to take an illustration from an advertisement, because possibly the art was sold for a specific use, and proprietary rights remain with the artist, as the ownership of a photo remains with a photographer. The use of an illustration from a publication under copyright is also improper. In the case of a desirable illustration under copyright, it is often possible to get permission to use it simply by asking. You might be asked to pay a small fee, if such work represents the originator's livelihood.

In the final analysis, producing one's own material is best in all respects, and it has the advantage of being specifically tailored to what is required of the product.

The present copyright law revision began January 1, 1978, and a copyright is now for the lifetime of the author, plus fifty years. Before revision, a copyright ran for two terms of twenty-eight years, and the copyright holder had to renew after the first twenty-eight year period.

PRESENTING THE ART

Presenting art for instant printing is as simple as making up the original to be reproduced. Whatever is represented to the camera as an image will reproduce on the printed piece; the original is the model for the finished product.

Many users present material to the instant printer in the same size and format that the finished piece is wanted in. For example, if the finished product is to be a flier on a sheet of 8½ × 11 inch bond paper, then the original is presented as an image on an 8½ × 11 inch sheet. If the image on the sheet of bond is a typewritten message, then the printed product will reproduce the typewritten sheet, looking almost exactly like the original.

It is helpful to realize that the surface the art is done on is really a matter of convenience, since only the image is photographed for the printing plate, not the surface. This in many cases makes it easier to prepare the image. It makes no difference to the camera or the process whether the image is one sheet or is made up of any number of different pieces pasted onto one sheet. The camera sees only the image and not the different pieces of paper.

When convenient, therefore, it is possible to use a larger sheet than the product size, indicating where it is cropped and composing all the material as separate pieces of paper. This technique is called paste-up, a widely used means of assembling art. The paste-up technique makes it easier to compose and position the various elements of copy and art for the best effect. It makes it possible to shift various blocks of typewritten material around to find their best positions, an impossible task on a typewriter.

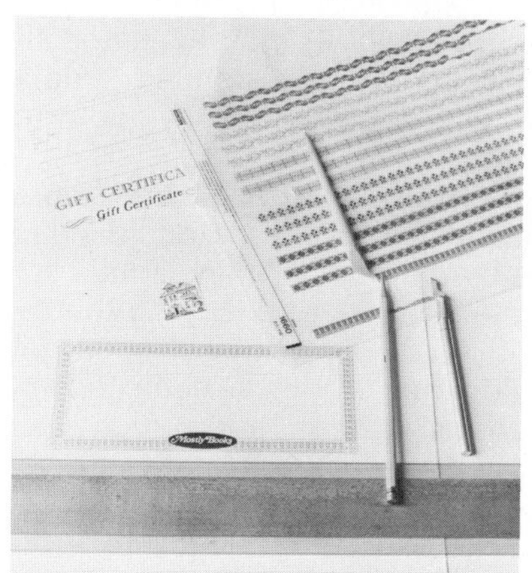

3-7. The partially completed paste-up will be finished as a gift certificate design. The type proof is at the upper left, the transfer type borders at the right, and the art below in the middle. The borders have been transferred, and the logo placed over the border. The straight edge at the bottom of the paste-up is the center section of a T square.

GIFT CERTIFICATE

Mostly Books, 4016 Wilshire Boulevard, Los Angeles, California 90010
will redeem this Gift Certificate for merchandise in the amount of:

Amount ______ Date ______

To ______ From ______

Address ______ By ______
Authorized By

Mostly Books

3-8. The paste-up, when completed, becomes this certificate.

The traditional adhesive used to attach these pieces of paper to the mounting surface is rubber cement, favored because it dries quickly and because any excess is easy to remove and clean up. It is available from any stationery or art supply store. The small bottle of rubber cement has a brush attached to the top, like a bottle of nail polish. The technique is to brush the cement on the back of the piece to be stuck down. The piece is then positioned and slid the last fraction of an inch to the correct alignment. In about a minute, when the rubber cement is dry, the piece is stuck into position. Any excess rubber cement is rubbed lightly off, because it attracts dirt, becoming dark enough to photograph along with the art image.

Other adhesives are more difficult to handle. Double-sided tape will work, for instance, but there is a risk of snagging the art at the corners, since it does not hold the entire surface down. Various pastes and glues can also be used, but many are so wet they warp the paper.

One of rubber cement's virtues is the ease of removing a piece that has been stuck down. A little rubber-cement thinner releases the bond, and then the piece can be repositioned and remounted with more cement. Thinner does not warp the paper.

Wax adhesive is also popular for paste-up. It retains its tack, as soft wax would, for an indefinite time. But when the attached piece of paper is burnished, it bonds tightly. In some ways it is even easier to use than rubber cement, but it needs to be heated and rolled onto the back of the mounting paper with an applicator, often too big an investment for intermittent use.

Type proofs may be ordered with wax backing, and many other graphic materials can be purchased with adhesive already in place, such as mounting and transfer sheets. These release

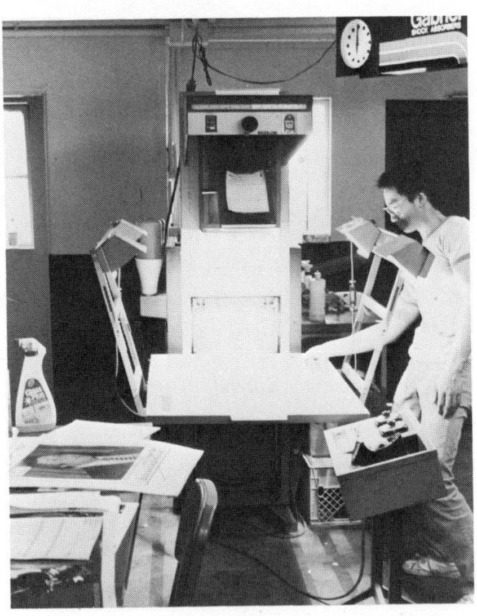

3-9. Only the crisp black image of the art will be presented to the camera when the printing plate is made.

with rubber cement thinner.

A special, high-tack, one-coat rubber cement allows working techniques similar to those of wax. Many find the kind in an aerosol spray can most convenient and this dispenser is also better for intermittent use.

A heavier mounting board is usually preferred over bond paper for paste-up. Ledger and bristol pads provide a suitable weight for small paste-ups, as do index board and railroad board. Larger sizes require an even heavier stock to prevent flexing, which tends to make the mounted pieces pop off. Heavier boards, also easily available from an art supply store, are mounting board or illustration board.

Many people protect the finished paste-up by keeping it in a file folder that matches the format sizes of instant printing. In any event, it is best if the art for reproduction is kept clean with some kind of protection; a covering flap of tracing paper prevents dust, dirt, and smears from spoiling the finished product.

The paste-up technique in one of its many variations is the easiest way to compose the elements used to produce art for instant printing, and a crisp, clean original of sharply contrasting black and white produces the best-quality printed product.

SHORTCUTS

In making up the original art for instant printing, there are important shortcuts in technique employed to produce the finished product more easily. Users of instant printing are sometimes more concerned with the quality of the product design than with saving time and work, but shortcuts improve quality by making the work simpler. Quality of paste-up like most crafts, even though done with the finest materials, is helped by a certain amount of practice.

Mounting the individual elements of the paste-up in exactly the right positions is made easier by cutting the edges true in the first place. Then the optical effect from the edge does not fool the eye.

With practice, the ubiquitous artist's knife and cutting board are usually easier and faster than scissors. The advantage is that cuts can be made along a metal straightedge, so they are true.

A T square, used on a drawing board or on the straight edge of a table or desk is almost indispensable for achieving an exact alignment.

Another technique for aligning things that has gained favor is the use of a mounting board with a grid printed on it in non-reproducing blue. The horizontal and vertical lines are a great help in positioning the separate elements of a paste-up. A light table can also be employed, permitting use of a grid *under* index, bristol, and ledger boards.

Adhesives continue to improve. Easy-to-use dispensers, small quantity, and low price are features. One is wax stick from

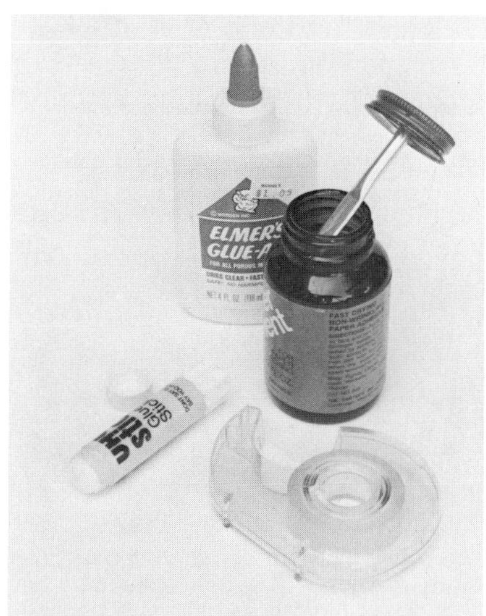

3-10. All kinds of adhesives are used to make a paste-up for instant printing. but the small bottle of rubber cement at the center is perhaps the easiest and least expensive. Wax adhesive is more expensive, but many find it the most desirable as a paste-up adhesive.

which the wax is dispensed from the end, like a lipstick, and rubbed onto the back of the piece to be stuck down. This provides all the convenience of wax for small jobs, without a waxer. The tack of the wax, though, is not sufficient to keep a mounted piece from falling off if there is any flexing of the board. A glue stick, similar to the wax stick, is also available. It is water soluble, but not so wet that it warps paper. When dry, though, the glue sticks permanently, and the paste-up piece cannot be removed.

Adhesive that keeps its tack like wax or one-coat rubber cement undoubtedly provides a faster method of paste-up. When the entire back of the paste-up material is coated before cutting, no clean up is required. The entire back of the sheet is coated with adhesive and then placed against a surface from which it can be lifted. This surface is used as a cutting board. With planning, all the cutting can be done at one time, and the separate pieces don't fall off the board.

Illustration board can be used as a cutting board. Other surfaces, such as vinyl, glass, and plastic or formica, can also be used as non-stick cutting surfaces from which the adhesive-backed pieces can be peeled. The material should not be burnished down on the cutting board, since it is difficult to remove without thinner.

Working at the same size as the finished piece is better, because it is easier to gauge the final effect. Reasons for not observing this rule are when all the original art is oversize or when fine detail makes it necessary to work larger.

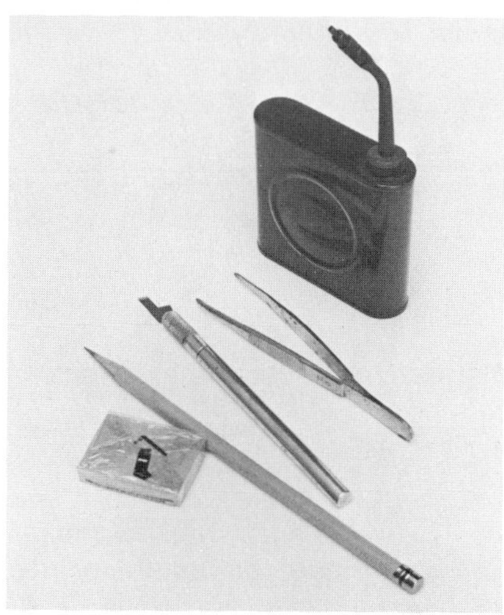

3-11. A few simple tools make doing paste-up easier. The oil can controls the amount of rubber cement solvent used to loosen a piece of paper already pasted down. The tweezers are handier than fingers. The artist's knife and non-reproducing pale blue pencil are indispensable. And the kneaded rubber eraser, shown in its cellophane package, makes clean up easier.

An oversize, finished paste-up is photographically reduced for printing. Reduction or enlargement can also be used to change from one product format to another of different size or to make incorrectly proportioned material fit a product format. It is always preferable to reduce the art because this makes the image sharper and reduces imperfections.

Typewriter ink, carbon, or copier images should not have adhesive or thinner on them or be smeared, because the image will be destroyed. Because these images are delicate, it is usually easier to handle them after they have been protected with plastic fixative. Be sure to spray lightly at first; otherwise, the solvent in the fixative will dissolve the image.

Burnishing to stick the adhesive-backed pieces firmly to the mounting board is always done over a protective sheet, and the "siliconized" sheets that protect transfer materials are especially useful for this purpose.

The inevitable corrections are more easily made by placing new material over old. It is faster to handle larger rather than smaller units. Corrections, such as one letter in a misspelling, are easier to make if the copy is redone to the end of the paragraph.

Removing delicate images, which can be blurred with rubber cement solvent, is easier to do with a metered flow of solvent from an oil can or by dipping a brush into the solvent. The thinner is applied at the edge, and then as the edge comes loose, the solvent is worked across the underside. Starting at the top edge on a slightly-tilted table is easiest. Tweezers will keep adhesive off the fingers.

Photostats may be used to change size, to make color corrections, or to provide a sharp print for the paste-up that is to be used for instant printing.

A copier that produces an image with a clean edge can sometimes be used on color copy by manipulating the copier contrast to provide a sharp image in black and white, which will reproduce better.

Development of an aesthetic sense, along with skill, comes with practice. A signal that this is happening is a continuing improvement in product quality.

COPY 4

Copy refers to the written material that goes into the instant-printing product. After it is incorporated into a paste-up as a graphic image, the instant printer may call it "art-copy," since pictures are included along with the type.

The copy used for the product is made into a graphic image in a variety of ways; the simplest is done by typewriter. The most basic use of instant printing is the duplication of the typewritten page. The type image can also be produced with the composer, transfer type, drawn letters and typesetting. These methods present an ascending order of graphic quality. Of course, the conventional way to turn written material into a type image for printing is with typesetting. It heads the list for quality and variety in handling the graphic image of copy, and it is necessarily more complicated and expensive than using a typewriter.

These different methods may be used in a variety of ways to design and make up the product at the level of quality and cost required for instant printing. The user selects according to the design requirements. In all cases the copy image is handled as paste-up to make up the art for the product.

4-1. The graphic image for the copy is produced by typing or typesetting. The interchangeable type fonts used in a composer set type in a way that is rather like typing, though it is really typesetting. Instant printing copy is an excellent application of the composer.

TYPING AND THE COMPOSER

When typing is used instead of typesetting to make the art for instant printing, it may be done simply by typing the material in position on a piece of paper. Often it is too difficult to figure out the space required and to position the typing correctly. The typing, therefore, is done on separate pieces of paper and then assembled as paste-up to make up the product.

4-3. By using a non-reproducing blue line at the margin typewritten lines can be made in end more evenly. The blue pencil is placed in the notch on the shield and held against the paper, while the platen is rotated to mark the margin.

Mechanical Typewriter

Electric Typewriter

Typewriter with Carbon Ribbon

Changeable Typing Element

Proportional Spacing Typewriter

Typesetting with A Composer

4-2. Starting with the least desirable type image at the top, the images progressively improve. The composer allows the combining of different typeface designs. The typewriter with proportional spacing has a typeface in place of typewriter type.

To use a typewriter to make the type image for instant printing, it is important to provide the best possible conditions. At the very least, a fresh ribbon and bright, white paper should be used. The typewriter keys should be clean, so that every letter is readable. An electric typewriter is a better choice than a manual one, because the even pressure produces an even blackness of the letter. A carbon-ribbon is preferred over a fabric ribbon, because the letter image of the former is blacker and has a cleaner edge. The interchangeable fonts of some typewriters provide a choice of typefaces, so it is possible to pick the one most suitable for the product. Proportional-spacing typewriters produce better spacing than the unit-space typewriter. Proportional spacing produces an image rather like typesetting with different widths for wide and narrow letters. Some of these machines even offer a variation on a typesetting typeface, instead of having only typewriter designs.

The normal typewriter techniques certainly apply in preparing material for instant printing. The margins are positioned on the left- and right-hand sides, but typewritten copy is flush left and ragged right in configuration. The line length is ended after the bell sounds.

Line lengths of a shorter measure can be used to divide

Typing can be done to a narrow margin
margin more easily by first drawing a margin line. The words that
run over the line will be cut away
away for the paste-up.

Typing can be done to a justified
margin by making two typings, the
first to count the letters in the
space, and the second to add/////
space between the words and position the letters.

Typing can be done to a justified
margin by making two typings, the
first to count the letters in the
space, and the second to add
space between the words and position the letters.

4-4. With the correct margin established, typing can be done with line endings not exceeding the desired measure, as in the top paragraph, where the blue line is indicated in black. The dotted line shows where the cut is made for paste-up. The following paragraphs show how to do justified typing.

the page into columns for easier reading and an alternative design. One easy technique to make the line end on the right-hand side more precisely than with the bell is to draw a line at the exact width required with a non-reproducing blue pencil. The left-hand margin is set; the width is measured; and then the pencil point is held against the paper while the platen is turned. The line is typed until it approaches this penciled margin, when either the word is broken with a hyphen or restarted on the next line. Unwanted words or letters are cut off the paper before it is mounted in the paste-up.

Some typesetting effects can be approximated with typewriter type and a little ingenuity. For instance, the small letter "o" can be blacked in with ink and used for a bullet • at the start of a line of type. A ballot box □ may be approximated by using the underscore together with the slash. Horizontal rules can be indicated with the underscore. More decorative rules and display boxes may be made with the asterisk *, number sign #, or mathematical symbols + and =. The hyphen and period can also be used for leaders and rules - - - - or . . . . .

Boldface can be imitated by repeatedly typing over the desired words to make a blacker-than-normal impression, but it must be done with care to keep the effect uniform. Perhaps it is easier to use typewriter techniques and substitutions instead and to indicate boldface or italics by underscoring.

With two different typewriters or two different fonts, additional designs are achieved in assembling a design for a product. Other variations can be gained by using a copier for reduction and combining the small and large images. The two different sizes of typewriter type, pica and elite (the equivalent of 11 point and 10 point type sizes respectively), can also be combined to good effect.

Rather than striving for a great many special effects on a typewriter, the more direct approach of using typesetting may sometimes be simpler, less laborious, and at the same time more effective in design.

Typesetting can be done on a composer, a machine that looks something like a typewriter, though it has more controls. It offers a variety of typeface designs and variations in size for text type.

Mechanical composers set type in the same manner that a typewriter types and are easiest to use with a flush-left, ragged-right configuration. They can also be used to justify columns of type where both left-hand and right-hand margins are straight, but this requires two typings on a mechanical composer: one to count the space and the other to position the line. For this reason they are generally used with the same flush left and ragged right configuration as typing.

Typing can also be done with both right and left margins straight, that is justified. This also requires two typings, one to count and the second to place the line. The difference is that the composer makes the count mechanically and equalizes the space, while typing for justification requires the typist to make the count and only partially distributes the space. On the computer-driven composer the type is automatically justified, and once the input of key strokes is recorded, the computer-controlled printout is done at something over one hundred and fifty words a minute.

• Bullet (o filled-in)

/_7 Typewritten Ballot Box

(_) Typewritten Ballot Box

____

**********-----------++++++++++

. . . .

4-5. These examples show some favored methods to simulate typesetting characters not included on the typewriter. Substitutions can also be made for rules and leaders.

Typing can be done to a justified margin by making two typings, the first to count the letters in the space, and the second to add space between the words and position the letters.

IBM Courier 12 type is a square-serif design in the Elite family of type styles and is similar to the Courier 72 element.
ABCDEFGHIJKLMNOPQRSTUVWXYZ []@#$%¢&*()_+ 1234567890
abcdefghijklnmopqrstuvwxyz -=°!:;"',,..?/

IBM Courier Type is a fine line, square-serif type style. It can be used for a wide range of typing applications.

ABCDEFGHIJKLMNOPQRSTUVWXYZ @#$%¢&*()
abcdefghijklmnopqrstuvwxyz -_=+½¼'";:/?.,
1234567890

4-6. The size of the typewriter image can be adjusted either by resizing with a copier or by choosing between the elite and pica typewriter type. The top image is a 75 percent reduction of the largest pica size of typewriter type; the next is the elite size; and finally the pica size.

Some computer-driven word processors also produce justified columns. The type image is obtained in a number of ways, depending on the machine design, and the resulting image is roughly equivalent to a carbon-ribbon electric typewriter. The word processor's main advantages are the greater speed and the ease of composing and printing out the typewritten image.

The composer is ideally suited to the requirements of instant printing. The carbon-ribbon, strike-on image is sharp and black, as well as suitable for getting the best quality of reproduction. The choice of typeface design, spacing, and the variations in typesetting techniques make it possible to produce designs with a professional look, while at the same time providing the greatest economies.

The typewriter and the composer both provide only the sizes of type necessary for text. Display headings are usually done separately with transfer type, but they can also be drawn. Another technique for display type uses a photostat that reverses the image into white letters against a black background. The letters are cut out in a panel, and the black panel with white lettering is used as display.

When designing something, labor is measured against cost, and these are kept in proportion with the effect wanted in the finished product. Instant printing can be done with any image that is provided. The choice of typewriter, composer, or typesetting equipment is dependent on the desired effect. The finer methods produce finer results, but at higher costs.

In the last analysis, typesetting for instant printing can be done in a simple way to keep costs low. The typewriter can be used effectively to produce a design. The composer adds the qualities of typesetting to the possibilities for design. By doing display headings in transfer type, the total effect approximates that of typesetting at the lowest cost.

TRANSFER TYPE

The use of transfer type provides an easy, inexpensive substitute for a small amount of typesetting. Display headings and designs for instant printing can be created with it, and the varying sizes it comes in can be used to supplement typesetting with a composer or a typewriter.

Transfer type can be bought from art supply stores and from stationers in sheets of letters and numbers with punctuation marks. Catalogs show literally hundreds of different type styles and sizes along with ornaments, art, and art aids.

Improved adhesives have made it possible to print letters on a carrier sheet and coat them with adhesive for transfer onto a mounting surface. The tack on the letter is greater than the tack on the carrier sheet, so that when pressed onto the mounting surface, the letter adheres to the surface and releases from the sheet.

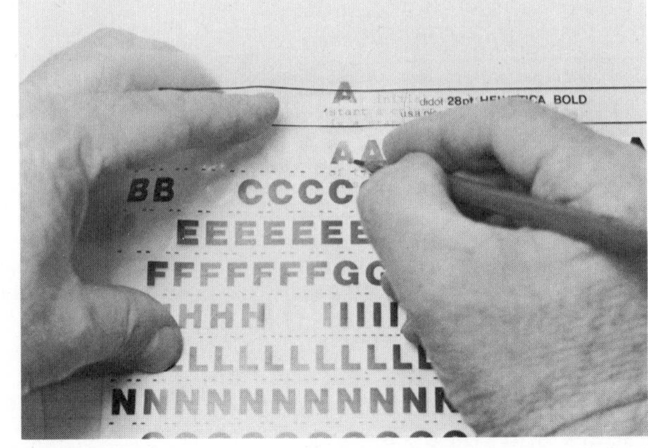

4-7. Transfer type can be used to make display headings for instant printing art. This type is the kind that is transferred to surface of the art by pressure on the carrier sheet. The empty ball-point pen makes a good stylus for rubbing the letter. Don't press harder than necessary. When the letter is released, the surface becomes dull gray instead of clear black.

Most kinds of transfer type work this way, but another variety has the letters permanently adhered to a transparent transport sheet. This sheet is cut, and each letter is placed on the mounting surface, with the transport sheet overlying it. Each kind of transfer type has its virtues. The directly transferred letter, like a decal, leaves only the image in place, but it cannot be moved once it has been transferred. On the other hand, the letter attached to the transparent transport sheet can be lifted and repositioned to adjust spacing before being burnished down permanently.

The manufacturers give instructions in their catalogs on how to use their products. The transferring and burnishing of the letters on a mounting surface is basically very simple. The art of doing it well, though, comes with practice.

For a heading with transfer type, the type design and size is decided, and the sheet purchased. Then a base line is drawn, on which to align the letters. If it is drawn in non-reproducing blue, it does not have to be removed before printing. It can be used with the alignment guide on the letter sheet, or it can be used at the base of the letters. Working from left to right, the letters are positioned one at a time to spell out the words of the heading. The choice of which kind of transfer type to use may well depend on the spacing requirements of the design.

It is very useful to draw out the design before transferring the letters. This can be done on a separate sheet of paper or in non-reproducing blue in the space where the letters are to be placed. Drawing the letters first reveals letter spacing problems. It also indicates the spelling of the word. When concentrating on letter spacing and design, it is easy to misspell a word. The type is transferred from left to right, producing a straight left-hand margin and a ragged right-hand one. Letters can also be positioned from right to left, but this is more difficult, because we are used to working in the other direction.

An initial can be used to start a column of typing. This is a stand-up initial

An initial can also be used as an inset into the column of type, and uses less space in this style of design.

4-8. Transfer type is used with the typewriter in other ways that simulate typesetting. These are two styles of initial openings.

It is impossible to estimate the exact length of a line or word before the letters are actually in position. If they are transferred to a separate sheet of paper, instead of being placed directly on the art, they can be repositioned in the paste-up. The lines can then be centered or moved to new positions to adjust the spacing. A virtue of transfer type is that individual designs are under the direct control of the user. For example, type can be spaced tightly, or openly, according to preference.

Designs that call for drawing the base line in a circle or in a curve are more of a challenge to space. Transfer type that releases can be used in a circle, where, after each letter is placed and it is seen how far around the circle it reaches, the paper is cut and the type repositioned. Transfer type on the transparent transport sheet is usually easier to use with a curving base line, because of its having letters that can be adjusted for spacing.

Transfer type also offers rules and embellishments to be used in typographic designs. Initials can be used both with typesetting and with typewriter type. An initial may stand up on the first line and be indented or flush left. The embedded initial takes more planning to get the following lines of text to fit around it. The block design of initial letter, when appropriate, is easier to handle, because it only requires counting the indent for the correct number of lines to run around it.

Some of the typographic devices available on transfer type are circled numbers, ballot boxes, stars, and bullets among others. When these are used with typewritten copy, they make it much more flexible and the finished result more attractive.

Though this kind of type comes in an immense assortment of designs and sizes, the exact one may not always be available. This problem can be solved by doing the heading on a separate piece of paper to adjust position, or failing this, the heading can be reduced to a smaller size on a copier.

With ingenuity letters can be positioned and combined with ornament to make up logo designs and other special effects. The primary use of transfer type for headings requires only aligning the letters and equalizing the space between them. Practice will develop a finer control of spacing and the pleasing aesthetic effects that can be obtained this way.

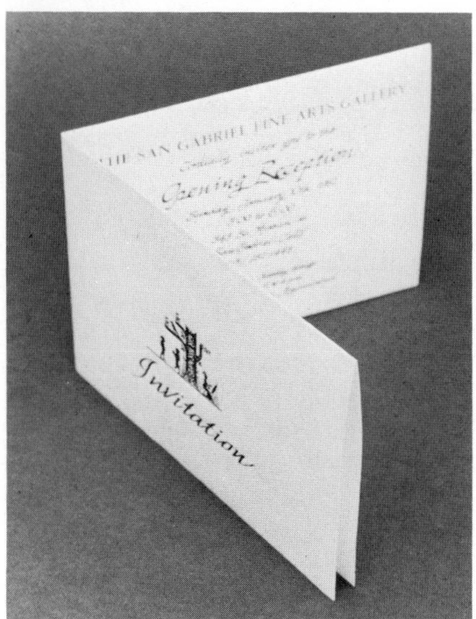

4-9. Calligraphy can be used in combination with other type images for some products. Most of us have a style of block lettering used for filling in forms that can serve in place of calligraphy.

DRAWN LETTERS

Drawn lettering is another way of doing typography for instant printing. Everything at its inception is drawn to produce the prototype, and drawn lettering is popular for use with instant printing among those who have the hand for it. In advertisements in the past, much of what appeared to be typography was actually hand-lettered art. The skills required to design and render the lettering were those of specialists. In comparison the kind of drawn lettering used for instant printing is much more casual, less exacting, and time-consuming, but still very effective in some applications.

Calligraphy, the art of beautiful handwriting, takes much practice for proficiency. Those who are accomplished in it often find it useful for instant printing invitations, certificates, or menus, for example. Drawn letters in contrast to calligraphy have a more universal application in headings. The letters can follow the form of typography, or they can be styled and interwoven into a design. When done casually as they often are, they will have a lighter appearance, something like cartoon lettering.

After filling in all the forms we do, most of us have developed a block-letter alphabet that is a substitute for handwriting. This can also sometimes be used for instant printing. Larger lettering for display headings can be derived from the same approach. What some people do is to borrow from the lettering in a catalog, freely tracing the outline of the letter and adding such styling as needed.

One good technique for doing lettering is taken from the cartoonist. After parallel guidelines on which to place the letters are drawn, the letters are first formed in non-reproducing blue. When the drawing is satisfactory, the letters are gone over in ink. The blue will not reproduce, and only the ink lines will show in the finished product. The same technique of preliminary drawing can be done in lead pencil, of course, but it will have to be erased. This requires a suitable paper surface, a kneaded eraser to disturb the ink lines as little as possible, and an ink that resists the eraser. White paint is used to correct the ink lines.

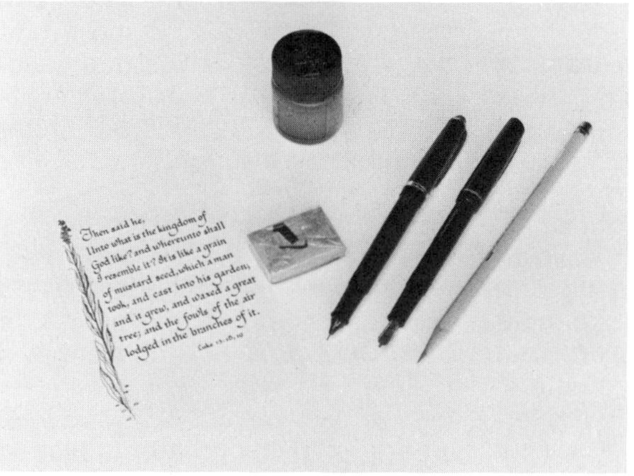

4-10. The art shown with the pens is a quote card done in calligraphy with a chisel point pen. The different sizes of letters required two widths of chisel, and the art at the left was done with a drafting pen.

Suitable materials for drawn letters improve the final result. Calligraphy makes use of a variety of pens and nibs, such as the chisel-point nib for thick and thin strokes. Drawn letters can be done with any kind of suitable pen, and one of the most popular is the fiber pen, because it can be moved in any direction. Be careful that the ink doesn't smear or become too gray if an eraser is used over it.

Though lettering can be drawn with rules and guides for a more finished result, it requires a good deal of drafting skill. The casual letter, drawn freely with the flow of hand movement, more like calligraphy, is the easiest approach for many. A heading might be drawn several times to get a properly spontaneous effect. Some find that pasting together words or letters from several tries produces the best result.

Lettering done with a brush and ink is another way to create a heading, but, like calligraphy, it takes practice. The brush makes a characteristic stroke that gives a distinctive appearance to letters formed this way.

These techniques provide an opportunity for overlapping and interlocking designs that would be impossible with the standard letterforms of typesetting and transfer type. It is this that distinguishes the drawn design from one done mechanically. All the various approaches to drawn letters use drawing guidelines at the

4-12. Another form of calligraphy is lettering done with a fiber-pointed pen. Using tracing paper and tracing the letter forms will help the neophyte get display lettering almost as easily as using transfer type.

we're moving

4-13. The traced lettering can be reduced on the copier; the change in size will help clean it up.

base and top of the letters to help with alignment and spacing.

A technique for making drawn letters look more finished is to draw the letters in a larger size than the one they will be used in and then reduce them. A copier will do the reduction, though not when blue lines have been used, because they will show. In some cases, especially calligraphy, the entire design can be reduced for printing.

For good effect, drawn letters need not be done with mechanical precision. Rather, it is their relationship to the instant printing product and to the setting that makes for an effective use of drawn lettering.

4-11. To do calligraphy it is necessary to use a pen with a point designed for the style of lettering. A dense black ink and non-reproducing blue pencil for guide lines are also helpful.

TYPESETTING

Many people who want to use instant printing are unfamiliar with the graphic arts. They would use typesetting if they knew how, because the benefits in improved appearance are obvious. But it is not necessary to know anything about it to get the job done; the main requirement is to prepare the copy.

The typesetter does not write or edit copy, so he must know precisely what is wanted, down to the spelling and punctuation. Typesetting follows the copy sheet, just as instant printing copies the image that is supplied. Preparing copy may seem simple at first glance, but it becomes more difficult when the user discovers that it is necessary to make all the decisions about what the graphic product is to be and what it needs to say. A typewritten sheet is the best way to present copy for typesetting, so everything is legible.

With the typewritten copy sheet and the necessary information about the product and its size, the typesetter can produce settings of headings and text for the instant printing product. A typesetter can do much to improve the appearance of the copy with indents, margins, typefaces, positions, and sizes to make up a typographic design. It is best if the typewritten copy sheet shows the form wanted, so that the typesetter can follow it. Many instant printers have referral relationships with typesetters to help their customers. Some even have typesetting facilities on their premises.

The simplest way to buy typesetting is to take the typewritten copy sheet to a typesetter, explain what the product is to be and its size, and let him take it from there. The typesetter may suggest what typefaces and sizes to use and mark up the copy sheet or supply a type book,

4-14. These are type books that show examples of the designs and sizes of type a typesetter offers. The index of typeface designs might not mean much to the nonexpert, but seeing an example of a design makes it easy to pick out what is wanted. The large typebook is for the composer.

which displays typefaces and sizes to select from. In this case, with help from the typesetter as to which sizes to use to fit the design, it is possible for the user to do the basic planning.

The usual practice in buying typesetting for instant printing is for the typesetter to float the typesetting on a proof sheet. The user then cuts it apart and does a paste-up, positioning the type to make up the product design. It costs less to buy the typesetting only. When the typesetter does the design and positions the type to make up the product, it takes more time and costs more.

How much typesetting should cost is an open question. It is appropriate to spend as much on typesetting and art as for printing, but this standard varies widely according to print quantities and the complexity of the copy. It is safe to say, no matter how low the cost, that the product should be worth printing.

It is impossible to estimate typesetting costs without knowing the amount of copy and the requirements. With the copy sheet and specifications in hand the typesetter can give an estimate, at least within fifteen percent, of what the cost will be. Headings are priced higher and text copy lower, according to the technique used to produce the typesetting. For example, if an 8½ × 11 flier has an average amount of copy, one hundred words more or less, plus display heading, address, and telephone number, the total charge for typesetting should be in the same range as the cost for printing one thousand copies with instant printing. The cost for typesetting will vary with the sizes and changes in typeface, just as instant printing cost varies with different papers and additional steps involved.

There are several ways of limiting the expense of typesetting. The primary one is to present the typesetter with clean, concise copy and clear instructions to make the work easier and less time-consuming. For a further reduction in cost, have the typesetting floated for paste-up, not positioned or made-up into a design. Still lower costs are achieved by having only the text typeset or by using a composer to typeset the text. The headings are then done with transfer type or drawn letters, as previously explained. Text typesetting can be estimated at an average cost for an average line and can be done for a flier at near the typesetter's minimum charge.

When typesetting is done simply, or limited to the text, the costs are compatible with small quantities of instant printing. It does produce an attractive design, and in addition to appearance and legibility, there is the advantage that the same number of words takes up less space when typeset than typewritten.

When the beginner supplies the typesetter with clean copy and precise instructions, he or she must lean on the skills of the typesetter for mark-up. Apart from mark-up, a skill that takes

Then said he,
Unto what is the kingdom of
God like? and whereunto shall
I resemble it? It is like a grain
of mustard seed, which a man
took, and cast into his garden;
and it grew, and waxed a great
tree; and the fowls of the air
lodged in the branches of it.
LUKE 13: 18, 19

Then said he,
Unto what is the kingdom of
God like? and whereunto shall
I resemble it? It is like a grain
of mustard seed, which a man
took, and cast into his garden;
and it grew, and waxed a great
tree; and the fowls of the air
lodged in the branches of it.
LUKE 13: 18, 19

4-15. This is the same copy that was in calligraphy on the quote card, and it makes a comparison of size and legibility. Notice how much less space type takes for the same kind of readability. The typewritten portion would be an example of how copy should be presented to the typesetter for typesetting. The typesetting can follow the typewritten copy line for line.

much practice to learn, a layout can be used to explain what is wanted for the design. The layout is a drawing of the design, showing the various typographic elements in their size, position, and relationship with each other. The typesetter can follow a layout, even one done roughly, and interpret the sizes and typefaces according to the indication. This graphic method is the best way to get what you want. If this method is followed, along with the typewritten copy sheet, be sure that the typesetter knows that the type is to be floated for paste-up.

Typesetting provided to a retail client for use with instant printing is usually kept simple, with the choice of typefaces restricted to a few and the type set in a straightforward style. Everything possible is done to make things easy for the user untrained in the graphic arts. While this simplification is the common practice, it is important to remember that typesetting can be looked on as the artform of typography. There are many kinds of typefaces that may be made into attractive typographic designs.

No typographer offers every design made, but graphic arts typographers do have many of them, as well as the skilled typographers to do fine work, even at relatively low costs. Fine typography looks just as elegant in instant printing as elsewhere, and for the user of instant printing it is helpful to remember that while the exercise of taste doesn't increase the expense, it does help a good deal in producing an attractive and effective product.

ART 5

5-1. Clip art books are a fine source of art and decoration for instant printing work.

Most instant printing uses both pictures and words to communicate the idea. Art has the advantage of communicating more directly than words, so products that use art gain in effectiveness. In designing instant-printing products, the picture in some cases forms the foundation of the design. In fact, some products consist primarily of art using only a small amount of copy.

The decision to use art or type is a question of quality and effectiveness versus the cost to get the desired result. As type is set for the copy by a typesetter, so the art is done by an artist. Art for instant printing can be obtained in a variety of ways. Of course, those who are able can do their own illustrations and use their artistic talent to design their instant printing products. Others will employ an artist or photographer. Again, existing drawings can be used. Prepared clip art is very useful.

To get professional art quality, attract the reader, and communicate the idea, adapting prepared art is less costly than ordering original work. But handling prepared art makes a demand on the user of instant printing, because it is necessary to differentiate without the help of an artist between the various kinds of art and know how to use them on the paste-up.

To develop designs and select art, the user needs to distinguish between line art and continuous tone, such as that of photography. This distinction is necessary for art that is made to order as well as for already prepared art. Each form can be used for instant printing, but each needs to be handled differently.

LINE ART AND CLIP ART

Art composed of lines is the simplest form of art to use for instant printing, whether as original art or prepared clip art. It is for this reason that clip art is done as line art.

Line art can be recognized by its similarity to type. The key to it is that all printing areas are as black as printer's ink. Everything is represented as solid, definite line. And there are no gray-tone areas in the art, though some areas of lines may have a tonal appearance. The kinds of line art range from those using only outline to those with the effect of tone and texture. Techniques that use lines side by side or in cross-hatching can give the appearance of tone. By handling line in a variety of ways, the artist is able to achieve the look of various textures in tonal areas, representing such things as the bark of a tree or the folds of fabric.

Any line art, either original or clip art, can be used "as is" in the paste-up along with the typesetting. The instant printing process will register the image of the art in the same way as the type, reproducing what appears on the original. To be able to include art along with the copy is a great simplification and convenience, making it easy to judge in advance the result of printing.

When using the services of an artist for illustration, the illustrator needs to be presented with the requirements of the idea. A copy sheet can work as well in this case as it does for enlisting the services of a typesetter. In fact a user of instant printing, new to graphic art, should know that it is a normal procedure to use the services of a number of different people. Work seen in publications is the result of a collaboration by specialists, and so it is in instant printing. The user originates the work and chooses the steps that seem desirable or necessary to produce the kind of product that is planned. The user may start working on the idea with a copywriter, then employ an artist for illustration and a designer for the concept and assembly of the product, and finally hire the instant printer. More often, the user bypasses some of these steps in working out a product.

Clip art is obtained on transfer sheets, in books sold in art supply stores, and also in stationery stores, though in smaller supply. Books of it are handled by bookstores, and specimens can also be obtained directly from suppliers by mail order. Clip art is presented in convenient sizes so that it can be used right from the sheet by cutting it out. Line art can be reduced on a copier or with a photostat, if for some reason this is more convenient. Original art is often done

5-2. Line art can be done with outlines alone like the butterfly, or it can have an effect of tone like the drive-in movie illustration, where closer examination reveals the closely spaced lines that produce the effect of a tone. Compare this tone with the tone panel around the butterfly, which is a halftone screen. The screen makes a "soft register," not a tight one—it does not touch the lines. It would not matter if the butterfly were to move a fraction of an inch one way or another during printing of a second color.

at a larger size than will be used and reduced. Sometimes a border around the art will help control the size or spacing.

Line art is arranged with the type in the paste-up so that together they communicate the idea. Small art may decorate and enhance the message, while larger art will dominate the design and may be used to communicate the idea. An interesting relationship between pictures and words makes the design.

The use of clip art places the user in the position of selecting what is best for the design from what is available. This might be easier than thinking of an idea for an original illustration, though not so flexible. Art is often specific in what it conveys. Sometimes rather than trying to find a piece of art to fit a given design, it can be helpful to see if the prepared art suggests a way in which the product can be designed. It is an association of ideas that indicates how to write and design the instant printing product.

Pictures of particular business locations or activities are the preferred subjects for original art. It is not necessarily expensive to do original line art, nor is it difficult to find an artist to do this kind of work. There are many sources for generic clip art that can be used. The smaller quantity of art packaged on transfer sheets makes the purchase of clip art even lower in price. Line art adds a great deal to the effectiveness of an instant-printing product and nothing to the cost of printing.

5-3. The clip art of the butterfly, seen on the cover of the bottom clip art book, can be used in a variety of ways. It appears here on a notepaper design.

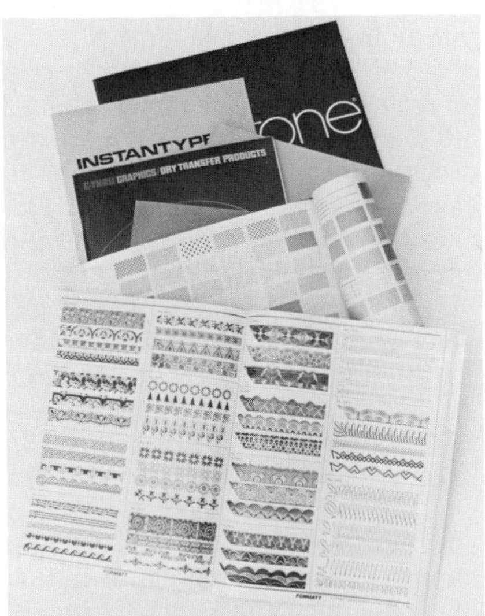

5-4. The dealer's catalog displays some of the many border designs and different kinds of tone sheets.

TONE SHEETS AND ART AIDS

Tone sheets and art aids are a great help in preparing material for instant printing. They can be used in designs for products, and they require only a minimum of artistic skill and craft.

Tone sheets and art aids are produced along with transfer type by the same manufacturers and are available at art supply and stationery stores. The many pieces of art that can be bought on individual transfer sheets are shown in manufacturers' catalogs. It is the illusion of tone that they give, for they are actually line art. The effect is produced by the small dots, which are solid black and suitable for printing. It is the size and density that provide the illusion for the eye.

Tone sheets are gauged as to darkness of value by the formation of the dot and as to density by the number of dots to the inch. The darkness is measured in percentages of black, so that white paper is 0 percent and solid black is 100 percent. The tone sheets are made in 10, 20, 30 percent, and so on, up to 100 percent. The density starts at 17.5 dots per inch and becomes finer at 30, 32.5, 42.5, 55, 60, 65 up to 85 dots to the inch. Fine screens, where the dot is less apparent, give a better illusion of tone than coarse ones. An 85-line screen, with 85 dots to the inch, is preferred for instant printing. An 85-line tone sheet would be used directly on the art. If the art is reduced by half for printing, a 42.5-line screen would come out to the optimum 85-line screen density for instant printing, when used at reproduction size.

The 10 percent dot on an 85-line screen is the minimum for safe reproduction with instant printing. Finer work than an 85-line screen can be done, but it depends on the tone values and the dot formation. With screens finer than 85 dots to the inch it becomes difficult for the process to retain the smallest dot, and some can be lost, speckling the screen and spoiling the effect of the tone.

The tone sheet is printed on a transparent, adhesive-backed sheet. It is lifted off the backing and rubbed lightly onto the art where tone is wanted. The normal alignment of the dots is at 45 degrees. The left-over part of the sheet is cut away and replaced on the backing sheet. The tone, applied on the art and cut to fit the outline, is then burnished to make it adhere permanently. In addition to tone sheets with black dots, there are ones with white dots to be used over black. There are also sheets with tone gradations to produce optical effects. Then there are sheets in textures with a variety of line patterns in place of dots. All these sheets can be used to give different tone effects to line art or to add backgrounds. They are also employed in borders, panels, and backgrounds for type. Tone gives a richer look to black and white art and produces unique treatments with clip art.

Art aids are individual pieces

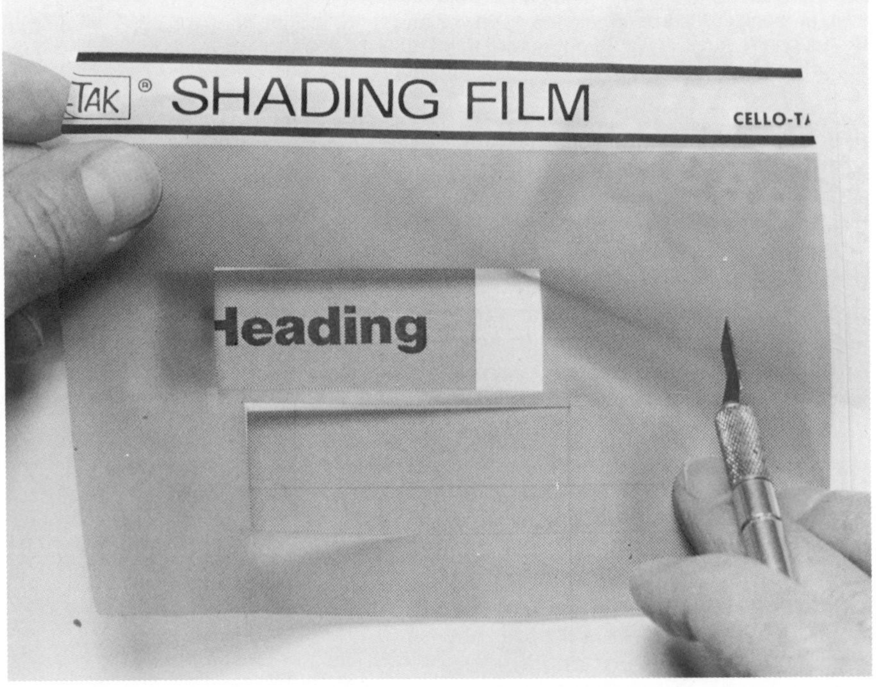

5-5. Tone sheets are handled this way. The light blue line underneath will not reproduce.

of art, useful in making up designs for instant-printing products. There are groups of numbers, arrows, rules, and borders. Symbols and ornaments come in different art styles, and there are small pieces of art. Cartouche shapes are available in a variety of sizes with different border designs. There are tapes that make black lines. Altogether hundreds of art aids are provided by different manufacturers to be employed in combination with each other and with transfer type, clip art, and tone sheets. They are used to design, decorate, or enhance the written message.

The increasing variety of art aids is a result of their popularity, and periodic changes take place as manufacturers change their product alignment. The art is of a high quality, some of it original and some reproduced from the best out-of-copyrght art-nouveau designs. Not only do art aids save time and effort, they also in their variety make it possible to produce unique designs with very little chance that anyone else will ever again combine the same art in the same way.

Tone sheets, art aids, transfer type, and clip art can be used by anyone, and the design for an instant-printing product is achieved by transferring these elements to a paste-up. Catalogs show in sample designs how each of the products is used. These art aids are prepared so that they can be either rubbed down, like transfer type, or transferred directly to the art, like tone sheets. The art elements need to be mounted cleanly, so that no dirt accumulates, because dirt will reproduce along with the art. This is especially true in handling tone sheets, where a speck of dirt underneath the sheet blemishes the reproduction.

Tone sheets and art aids make it unnecessary to draw anything. They provide instant art for instant printing and make professional-looking designs available to anyone who has the skill to combine the materials effectively.

5-7. The kind of transfer type where the image is attached to a transparent carrier sheet is handled this way and is perhaps easier to use when spacing must be adjusted. Along with type, there are art motifs, borders, corners, and transfer art to be used for illustration.

5-6. Type can be combined with tone sheets, both over and under the black type, but the reverse transfer type must of course be used on top. This tone is a 55-line screen with a 40% tone.

PHOTOS AND VELOXES

A velox is used to make it possible to print a photo. The term, velox, is really a trade name for high-contrast photopaper, but, like nylon, it has become generic. A velox is a halftone photoprint of tonal art.

To print a photograph, in which the tones extend through the full scale, the tonal values have to be made into a tone screen, like that of a tone sheet. The tones of a photograph are made into a halftone by rephotographing the photo-art through a halftone screen.

The halftone screen is composed of fine lines, similar to a window screen, with varying densities, like tone sheets. The way this works is that the screen is placed between the photo-art and the film, breaking the light into very small dots. The dots develop on the film, and the film is then photoprinted onto photo paper (velox paper), where the small dots produce the illusion of tone that corresponds to the photo-art.

The velox simulates the tone of the photo-art in solid black dots of varying sizes. Whereas the tones of the photo-art would be impossible to print in black ink, the varying dot sizes can be printed in solid black, thus reproducing the illusion of tone in the original.

For instant-printing paste-ups every piece of art that has tones of gray, such as wash drawings, must be made into a velox. If this is not done, the printing process will resolve the gray tones into black and white. Areas of dark gray will become solid black; areas of light gray will drop out, becoming white. Once the velox is made, the photo- or halftone art becomes line art, made up of small black dots, and can be used in the paste-up along with any other line art.

As line art the velox can be cropped, shaped, or be partially painted out with white or added to with black. Transfer type, both black and white, can be used directly on a velox, and the result reproduced. The instant printing process handles an 85-line screen. If a velox print is made with a finer screen, such as a 100-line or 110-line, the smallest

5-8. A photograph, like the one at the left, cannot be printed without using a halftone screen. The reproduction uses a 150-line screen, which is too fine for instant printing. The picture in the center (5-9) uses an 85-line screen recommended for instant printing. The picture at the right (5-10) shows how high contrast film will resolve the grays into black and white with the result that the light tones disappear. This photo was selected so that the shadows and hat would hold the shape of the face and detail of the features. With a different tone pattern the result of not using a halftone screen could be very disappointing.

5-11. This is the same photo with the background removed. It can be removed by cutting away the velox, or by outlining the image with white paint.

dots in the light tones may fail to print, leaving the halftone areas speckled with white.

There are several ways to obtain a velox. A reproduction service with a graphic arts camera supplies them. A laser scanner will also make a good velox, but with a different process. Some instant printers can supply a PMT halftone. The price varies according to the process used and to the size, with the break at 4 x 5 inches. It is helpful to know that the size of the photograph can be changed when it is made into a velox. The velox can also be cropped differently, when used in the paste-up for an instant printing product.

The best results with photography are obtained by enlarging directly from the negative, but the best results for a velox are achieved when the photo-art is reduced. This is because the photoprint is made from projected light, while the velox is made from reflected light. For this reason, use a glossy print with more reflectance to make a velox.

Since all photographs in print are halftones, it is on occasion possible to use them for instant printing. Reproduction of a 100-line screen is sometimes successful, because the dots have been made heavier by the printing process. It helps if the printed halftone is on a bright, light-reflective surface. The more distant the reproduction becomes from the original art, the greater the loss of quality. Newspapers printed by offset printing also use an 85-line screen in many cases, but results are variable, because the paper is not bright and the printing is of uneven density. Newspapers printed by letterpress use a 65-line screen and are easier to reproduce with instant printing.

Photography is another way of obtaining art for products without having to draw it. The quality of photography varies according to the ability of the photographer, of course, but anyone can take a snapshot for an illustration. With the additional steps of sizing and cropping for the paste-up, the design can be varied to produce the effect that is wanted.

When using photography there is the cost both of the print and of the velox for the paste-up. Instant cameras make it possible to shoot the picture and have the print immediately for the velox. Photography is a popular kind of art for instant printing products. In some instances, because of its literal quality, it is the best.

COLOR IN PAPER AND IN PRINTING

Instant-printing systems are based on the use of black ink. As the process departs from this to employ color, it begins to include the craft of custom work, adding to the cost. The effect of color is most easily obtained by using colored paper, which can be put on the press without altering the setup or adding to the labor.

An innovation, offered by some printers with at least two presses, is to run color specials. The basic retail format of one press running in black ink is maintained, while the second press duplicates this set up, but with a colored ink. It may, for instance, be red on Monday, blue on Tuesday, green on Wednesday, and brown on Thursday. On the busy days at the end of the week only black is offered. Color may be sold for the same price as black to encourage business activity on slower days.

Normally color is run at the end of the day, after the black ink is washed off the press. The customer is charged for re-inking in color and for washing up again. Work can be printed as color on white paper or color on colored paper. Two-color printing—first in color, then in black—can be done at double the cost. It is the practice in printing to charge the customer for the labor of putting the job on the press. Instant printing with its retail selling eliminates this charge as long as the job does not require custom work.

Color expands the range of ideas for instant printing products and enhances them. Despite the cost some product designs can only be printed in color, and others require two colors. The use of color may suggest a motif; black and white would be more symbolic.

Any design, however, that can be printed in black and white can also be rendered in color. Sometimes it is possible to achieve another effect for a design by printing in color on colored paper. For instance, the popular brown on beige may be

MOSTLY BOOKS HAS MOVED TO 645 SOUTH OXFORD AVENUE
(one block east of Western and just around the corner from Wilshire)

Our new hours are:
12:30 p.m. to 5:00 p.m. Mon. – Fri.
11:00 a.m. to 5:00 p.m. Saturdays

Our phone number is still (213) 388-1989

HOPE TO SEE YOU SOON

5-12. The promotional postcard with news about a move can be pasted-up tor two colors by using an acetate overlay. Or the art can be covered and shot separately to make two printing plates.

used to suggest an antique motif for a western theme. Or blue on light blue paper might imply a water motif for an aquatic theme. Color combinations that contribute to the design are as many as the imagination suggests.

Art for color is prepared in exactly the same way as for black and white. But the art should be in black and white. Preparing art in color makes reproduction difficult, because the process is intended to handle the greater contrast of black and white. Once the printing plate is made from the black and white art, printing can be done in any color on colored paper.

A second color can usually be added to any art prepared for instant printing in one color. This is done by selecting the part to run in color and the part to run in black, and one printing plate is made for each with two print runs.

To be able to make two printing plates from a single piece of art, the elements selected for color must not touch those that are to run in black. If a heading and border are to run in color, and the remainder in black, everything running in black has to be covered, while the heading and the border are exposed to make the printing plate. Then the procedure is reversed to make the black plate. After the second printing the piece would have all the elements of the original art, but in two colors. In two-color printing black is referred to as a color. The second printing could as easily be of any other color, but black is usually the choice for its strength.

When printing in color, it is important to note that color generally does not have the contrast that black does. This is particularly true where typography is to be run in color. What would normally be readable in black and white can become illegible in color on white or in still weaker color on color. Color would also

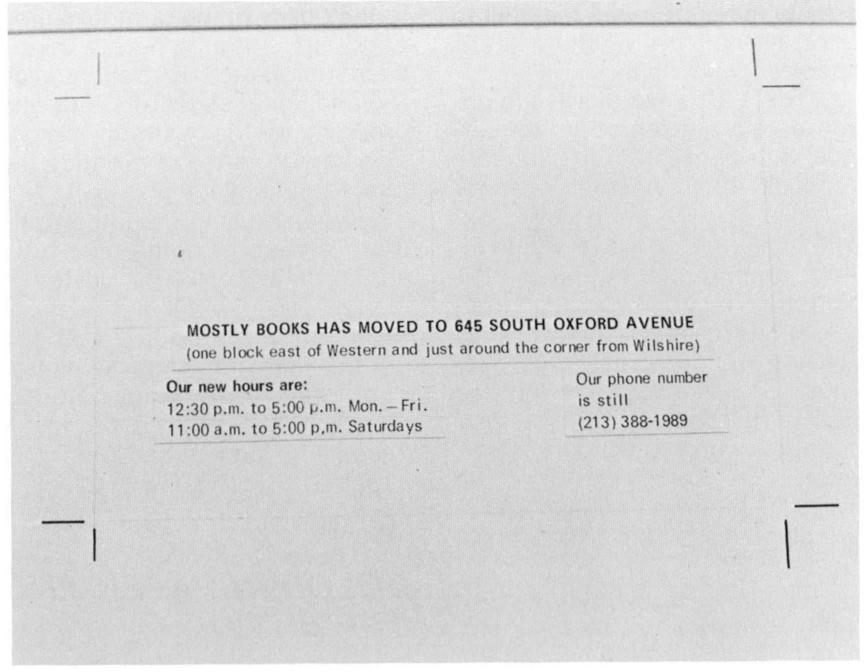

5-13. The art pasted on the main flat will run in black, shown here with the overlay lifted out of the way. Since the separate items of this design do not touch each other, the color portions of the design could be covered with paper. Note the corner crop marks that indicate the edge of the postcard.

5-14. The overlay is folded down, while the portion underneath is blocked from view by covering it with a piece of paper. A plate is made of this portion to run in color. Without the piece of paper the entire design could be photographed through the acetate. A strip of paper might also be cut to lay over the central portion of the design to block the part that is to print in black.

5-15. The portion of the design in gray is the color part of the two- color version of this design.

need to be used carefully on halftones and other art. Blue skin-coloring, for instance, would not look well. It also reduces the contrast of a halftone and may weaken a picture.

Colored inks are affected by the color they print over, because ink is transparent. Printing blue on yellow may produce a green. A common miscalculation is seen when the popular color red is screened back with a halftone or tone sheet, and the result of adding white paper to red ink is a weak pink. Colors can be combined effectively, but it is simpler for two-color printing to use a color plus black and white paper.

The press-feed used for instant printing limits the ability to register, that is, to position the second printing in exact relation to the first. There will always be a slight variation of about 1/64 of an inch and sometimes a little more. This doesn't sound like much, but when two colors must butt against each other, like a shadow line on a typeface, 1/64 of an inch will spoil the effect by letting a bright strip of white paper appear between the two colors. In cases where colors butt, they should overlap slightly. A much better plan for two-color instant printing, then, is to use art that does not need close registry.

Since the plates are made separately, the art for each color is prepared individually. The easy way to do this is to paste-up the art that is to run in black on one sheet and then to place a clear acetate sheet over it, positioning the color art on the acetate. The relationships of size and position and the effect of the overall design can be seen, but at the same time the acetate separates the art for the two printing plates. This standard method allows the printer to shield the black plate with a sheet of paper, while shooting the color plate. Next, the color art is lifted up and only the black plate exposed. The trick in preparing art for two-color printing is to know that each color is printed separately.

When preparing art for instant printing it should be noted that large areas of ink are difficult to print and require adjustments to the ink supply. In two-color art there is a tendency toward greater coverage, and some instant printers make an extra charge when more than 50 percent of the sheet must be covered.

Two-color designs are more complicated than black-and-white ones, but they offer more possibilities to enhance communication. Instant printers that provide color specials remove the objection to formats. They expand the range of instant-printing services on the week's slowest days and studies show that because color is 40 percent more effective than black and white, people want to use it.

PAPER 6

Paper contributes to the character and interpretation of a product by its appearance and tactile qualities. It forms an important part of the total impression. Paper is also chosen for its effect on sizing, folding, and binding. There are thousands of kinds of paper. It is a specialized field, and choosing the right kind requires a knowledge of how paper works with the instant printing process. It is necessary to be aware of how it takes ink and many other factors. The instant printing inventory of well-chosen paper stock spares the customer a great many problems.

Instant printing franchises purchase paper in large quantities and have succeeded in distributing to franchise holders at the right price because of high volume. The paper inventory is part of the retail service. They offer kinds that work well with the printing process and that provide for a variety of products. For cost and effectiveness their papers are hard to beat.

In special situations the customer can supply novelty paper, but it needs to be the format size and to be suitable for the ink on the press. It also adds to the job cost.

In general, papers used for instant printing have a delicate texture. They boast a finish that enhances the quality of the reproduction and that works with offset printing. Furthermore, within the range of the finish, texture, and weight that is offered these papers all accept a common ink. Instant printing can be done on other papers, even ones with a hard finish, like coated stock, but with less resolution of the image. Since ink is usually matched to paper, these papers require an ink with more gloss.

In addition to finish, it is also possible to select paper stock for instant printing according to quality or grade, weight, and color. The choices are determined by length of use—quality—and by product requirement—weight. Color is a matter of aesthetics. Envelopes are included in the stock.

6-1. The steps in making products out of printed sheets are broken down this way. Collating or gathering, folding and trimming, work in different sequences according to the requirements of the product. Drilling, stapling, and padding are all methods of binding printed sheets together.

6-2. Printers maintain a sizable inventory of papers. Although only three sizes are stocked, there is a variety of kinds and colors.

KINDS OF PAPER

The paper inventory stocked by the instant-printer might be broken down, as instant printing price lists are, into three kinds: bond, card stock, and specialty papers.

Bond is the basic paper for instant printing stationery, fliers, newsletters, and other products. The 20-pound bond used by printers can be substituted for text and book papers. It is usually stocked in at least two grades. One is a serviceable, all-purpose paper, and the other has a rag-content. When a paper needs to last longer or stand up to more handling, the rag-content bond is preferred.

Paper is made from fibers of different kinds, and the rag content has a longer, stronger fiber. The manufacturing treatment eliminates more of the acid content, so that it is less subject to yellowing and deterioration. Some art papers, for instance, are 100 percent rag content and are made to last several centuries. Ordinary papers yellow in a few years and begin to disintegrate after several decades, even when stored under favorable conditions. The average library book, for instance, has a shelf life of roughly fifty years.

The usual 20-pound bond has a serviceable quality, but the better rag bonds that are often watermarked have a refinement that makes an appeal to the senses. Some instant printers stock more than one kind, primarily for use as stationery, where the appearance and feel of the paper contribute to the product value.

Bond paper is stocked in as many as twelve different shades of red, yellow, blue, green, and tan. The better grades of rag bond are usually not stocked in colors.

The card stock in the inventory covers the range of index board, bristol board, and ledger board. It is essentially a heavy paper with a sizing or filler that makes it suitable for writing on with ink. It can be used for any product that requires a heavier-weight paper. Such things as business cards, note cards, or tags are made in this paper.

The same paper composition and weight can be made with a plate or a linen finish, for example. The card stock used by instant printers has essentially the same finish as bond paper, which is best suited to this printing process. It is carried in a variety of colors that match those of the bond papers.

Specialty papers in the in-

6-3. Six different kinds of paper all have approximately the same finish: (1) 20-pound bond, (2) rag bond, (3) dry gum, (4) contact adhesive, (5) parchment, (6) index board. The specific colors listed in one selection are tan, buff, green, cherry, gray green, goldenrod, salmon, pink, blue, ivory, and canary. Colors vary from printer to printer more than kinds of paper stock.

ventory are those used for a special-purpose product. Adhesive-backed papers, both dry gum and the contact kind, are examples. The printer may also stock parchment and a special-finish paper among others. The adhesive papers produce labels or stickers. Parchment can serve for certificates, and the heavier papers with special finishes might be used for cover stock.

There is nothing to prevent unusual uses of specialty papers. For instance, a flier could be designed in an antique style and printed on parchment for an effect. The same would be true of papers with special finishes, often used for pamphlets. Offset printing, employed in the instant printing process, handles textured paper easily because of the rubber offset blanket.

For the unusual product paper can be obtained from a jobber or from the inventory of an odd-lot supplier. Most paper is handled in bulk at the wholesale level, and this makes it difficult to obtain the small quantities used in instant printing, except as a remainder from some other job. Usually these specialty papers are in larger sizes for a bigger press and have to be trimmed to the 8½ × 11 inch format. An instant-printer will be able to trim a small amount of paper from some other source. Since instant printers add to their inventory from time to time by purchasing paper when there is enough demand, the user will find that the printer sometimes has papers that are different from the basic stock.

The environmental mandates have brought continuing increases in the cost of paper, as mills control the water pollutants used in the manufacture of paper. It can be seen from the price lists that a good portion of the cost of instant printing is for paper. Nevertheless, instant printing provides the labor-saving system to lower the price of many printed products.

SIZING AND TRIMMING

Sizes for instant printing products can be anything within the format of 11 × 17 inches. Smaller sizes are achieved by trimming products from the sheet size. Most items are designed to fit the sizes of 8½ × 11 and 8½ × 14 inches, because trimming is an extra step and adds to the cost.

There are additional format-sizes, which must be produced by trimming from an 8½ × 11 inch sheet. These are 5½ × 3½ inches for a postcard and 3½ × 2 inches for a business card. Perhaps the size of 4¼ × 5½ inches should also be included, because this is a popular size for note cards. It is one-fourth of the 8½ × 11 inch format, though there is no truly conventional size for note or greeting cards.

Except for small sizes instant printing permits going to the nearest format size and printing without waste or trimming. Odd-sized products are usually the result of the limitations imposed by the envelopes into which they must fit, and this requires additional cost for cutting the product to fit. Items such as tags, tickets, stickers, and bookplates must also be trimmed to size. They are printed in multiples on larger sheets and cut.

When a product is trimmed to size, a bleed edge is an option. In a bleed a picture, panel, or tone extends to the very edge of the page. The printing is actually done by extending, or bleeding, the material beyond the edge, the trim being inside the printed portion.

If printing is done to a format size with no trim, there can be no bleed. Art carried to the edge would result in ink transferring to the back of the sheet along this edge. A "false bleed" can be done only in small areas, such as a rule extending to the paper's edge, where there is not sufficient ink coverage to cause a problem. A full bleed to all the edges of a sheet, such as might be used in a catalog, can be achieved by printing to 1/32 of an inch beyond the edge and then trimming back ⅛ of an inch. The 8½ × 11 inch size becomes 8¼ × 10¾ inches. This is an acceptable solution for a one-of-a-kind product to gain the effect of

6-4. The printed piece is carefully measured and marked for trimming.

6-5. With the trim planned, the cuts are made swiftly with a powerful trimmer that zips easily through several inches of paper stock.

a bleed edge. Of course the printing has to be dry to withstand the pressure of trimming without transferring ink to the back of the top page, and ⅛ of an inch is normally the minimum that can be trimmed. If this is not done, the design should leave a margin on all sides.

Trimming is also desirable when a booklet is bound with staples. As the number of sheets increases, there is a "creep" at the outside edge of the booklet because of the thickness of the paper in the fold of the binding. With enough pages this creep requires an adjustment of the margin to equalize the center pages. With more than a half dozen pages, it is impossible to riffle the pages with the thumb, as we do with a book or booklet. To make this edge true the booklet has to be trimmed after it is printed, gathered, and bound.

Trimming separates the pages of a booklet, after it is bound. To avoid having to gather separate, smaller sheets, the pages of the booklet are printed on a large sheet and then folded and bound. After the booklet is bound, the pages are separated by trimming away the folds at the edge.

6-7. The edges of the center pages creep away from the binding of a booklet; trimming is the only way to get a straight edge.

6-6. The postcard design has a bleed at the head and both sides. The broken line shows where the trim will be. The corner crop marks, outside the art, indicate trim.

FOLDING

Folds are used to fit printed materials into envelopes or to construct pamphlets and booklets. The price for folds is based on a fixed rate for setting up the machine, plus an additional cost per hundred sheets for folding. This argues against folding less than several hundred sheets by machine.

Smaller quantities are better done by hand. The technique is to mark and measure the first sheet carefully, so that the folds are accurate. Then, with a rubber finger or glove and a burnisher the quantity is run through. The rubber finger positions the sheet, and the burnisher creases the fold. With this kind of mass-production technique a hundred sheets can be folded in a few minutes, and there is no need to pay for the machine. The cost is based on setting up two parallel folds, such as are used for a standard-sized letter to fit a number 10 business envelope. These same folds are employed to make up pamphlets.

The folds for pamphlets need to be positioned accurately, since the material in the pamphlet is generally designed in relation to

6-8. These are only a few of the many booklet designs that can be done with the instant printing format by varying the folding pattern. The two booklets at the top are half-sheet sizes done with folds in different directions on the 8½ × 11 inch format shown at the bottom. The booklet on top is one half of the 8½ × 14 inch format.

6-9. Heavier stock for the cover can be different colors, adding to the design of a booklet.

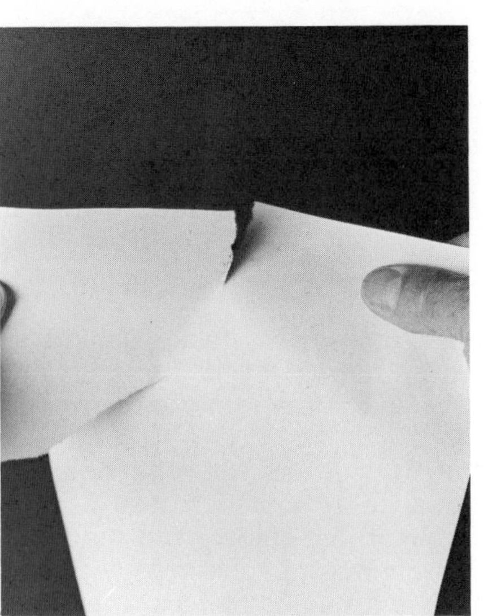

6-11. Tearing the paper from the side and top will reveal the direction of the grain. The tear from the side turned with the direction of the grain, but the tear starting from the top is running straight, indicating that the grain runs the length of the paper.

the crease. When a pamphlet has two folds and three panels, the panels are not exactly equal. The sheet that folds inside must always be shorter by the thickness of the paper, so that the second fold can wrap around the first without buckling the inside panel.

These same folds can also be used to make up booklets. The difference between pamphlets and booklets, of course, is that booklets have their edges cut after binding, so that the pages separate. Though a booklet needs to have its folds aligned accurately to position the pages, it has the benefit of trimming to remove any slight discrepancies.

The most common formats are two folds on the 8½ × 11 inch sheet for a pamphlet. The longer 8½ × 14 inch sheet can be folded in half and then in half again, giving four panels for either a pamphlet or a booklet. The largest 11 × 17 inch sheet can be folded in half to make a double 8½ × 11 inch sheet, and this folded sheet then can be folded in half again, like the 8½ × 14

6-10. After stapling, the side is trimmed by ⅛ inch to separate the sheets and complete the booklet.

inch sheet, or it can be folded twice in the opposite direction, like a letter. The French fold requires a fold in each direction.

The direction in which a sheet is folded is affected by the grain of the paper. It is always easier to fold with the grain, and styles that change direction always have one way that is more difficult to fold. In this case it is preferable to have the second fold run with the grain of the paper. Grain is determined by the direction in which the long fibers lie, and this can be discovered by tearing the paper in each direction. The straight tear indicates the direction of the paper grain. The direction is also usually noted on the paper package.

Folds may be made in many ways, even when working within an instant printing format of standard sizes, because reversing their direction produces a different design. Placing folds in upon each other is the most usual design, but the folds can reverse so that the design is an accordion fold, like pleats. When the direction of the folds is reversed, the pamphlet must be designed differently.

Booklets usually maintain the inward fold, with the individual sheets positioned head to head. It should be emphasized that a dummy must be made first, so that the sheet positions after folding and trimming are seen to be correct.

Another variety of fold can be used to make up a broadside,

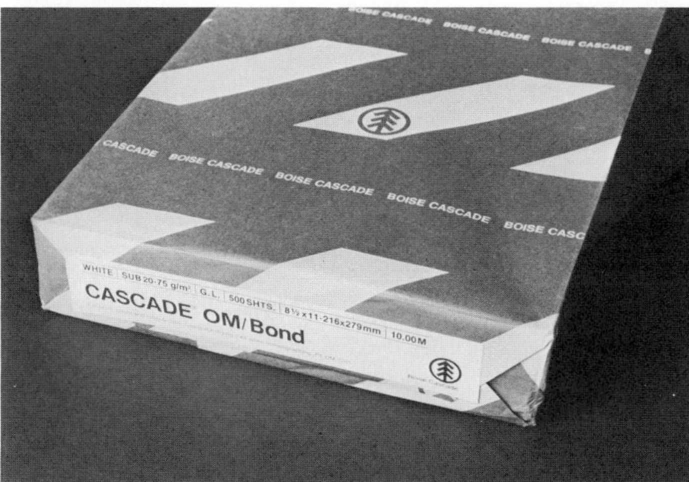

6-12. The paper package usually has the grain direction marked on the label.

WHITE	SUB 20-75 g/m²	G. L.	500 SHTS.	8½ x 11-216x279mm	10.00M

CASCADE® OM/Bond

For bond, offset and mimeo uses. Use quick drying inks when mimeographing. P1 OM 2201

Boise Cascade

6-13. The top line on the label has G.L. in the third box, indicating that the grain runs the length of the sheet.

though this is usually done on sheets larger than 11 × 17 inches. The broadside folds in half, then in half again in the opposite direction, and once more in half in the opposite direction. The end result will be 4¼ × 5½ inches. As the sheet unfolds, each new size is a separate design, and the final opening is the full sheet.

Pamphlets and booklets require printing on both sides of the sheet. For this reason the paper to be used should be tested to see how much the printing shows through the back of the sheet. It is also helpful to leave margins of at least ⅜ of an inch, so that slight variations of position in printing and folding are more tolerable. Tight margins make difficulties. Trimming a booklet also permits bleeds on the trimmed edges at no extra cost. Naturally margins are measured to the trim edge, not the paper edge, and the design is planned for the way it will look after trimming.

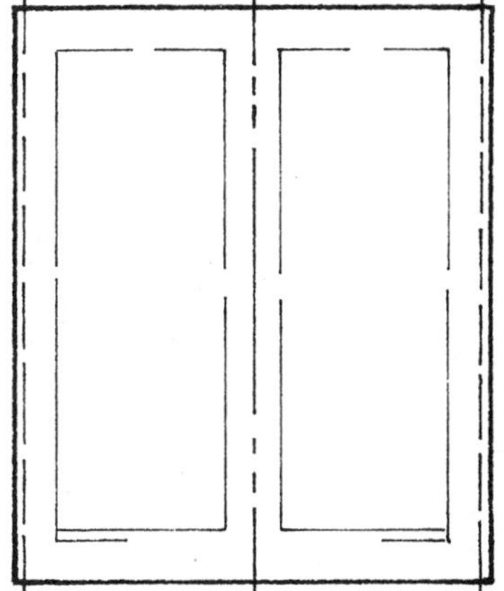

6-14. With ⅛ of an inch trimmed from the edge, the margins are moved inward to the center fold on each sheet to compensate, as indicated here by the broken trim line and margin format.

BINDING

The instant printing methods of binding are stapling, padding, and drilling, and some printers also offer special plastic bindings. Booklets may be held with stapling; forms can be bound into pads held with glue; loose sheets may be drilled for a ring binder or bound into a book with a spiral binding.

The stapled binding lends itself to a large variety of booklet designs. A number of separate printed sheets can be gathered to create booklets with papers of different weights and colors. Other materials, such as return cards, can be added and bound in with the other sheets.

6-15. The wire rolls at the end of the collator feed into the stapler, which fastens the gathered sheets.

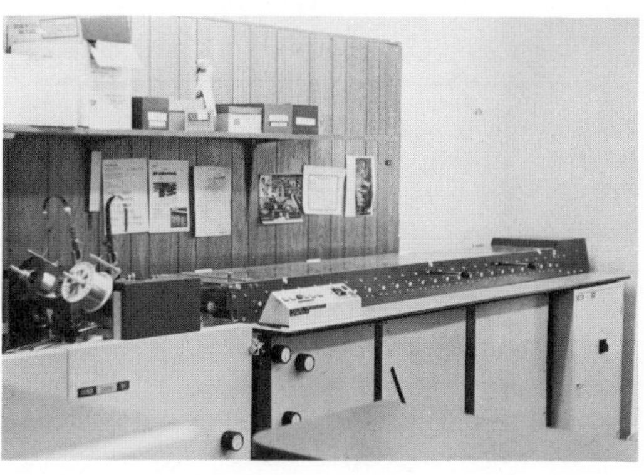

6-16. A different view of the collator shows the many sheets that can be gathered into one booklet.

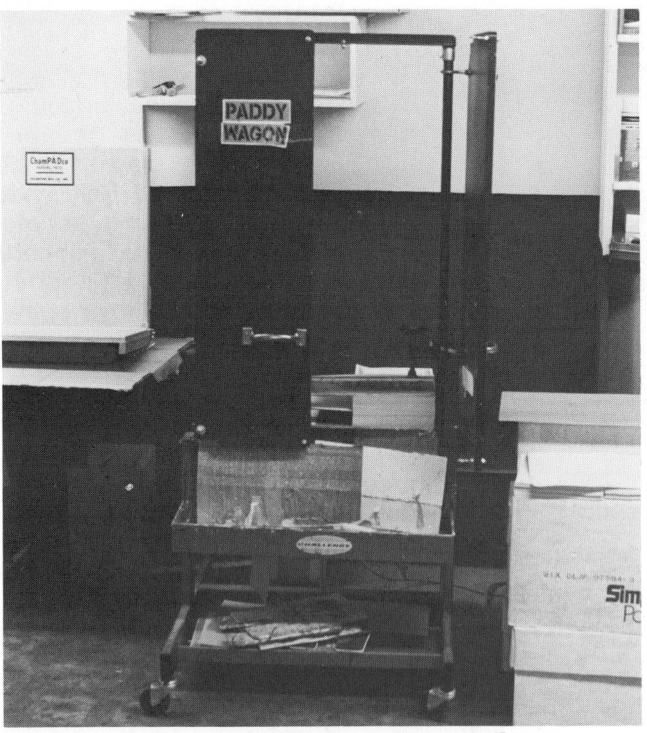

6-17. Padded stock is held under the clamp on the "Paddy Wagon" to allow it time to dry.

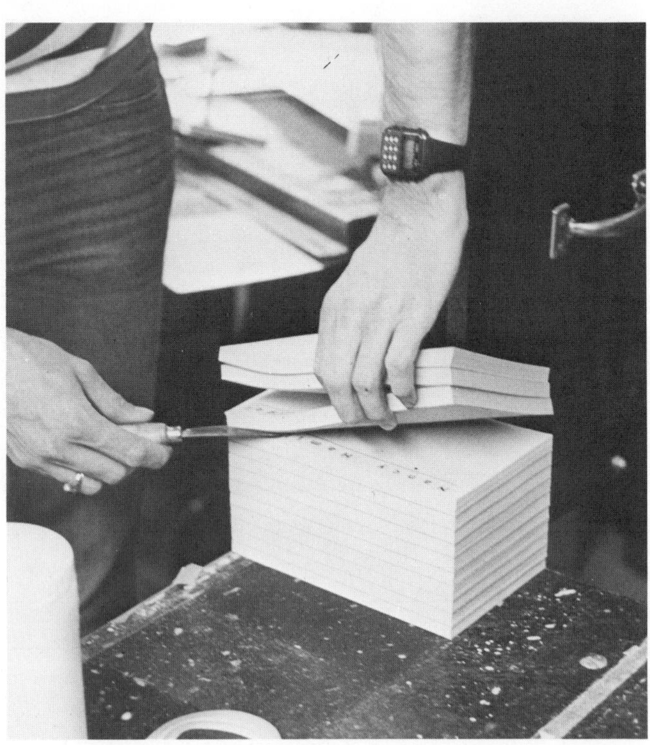

6-18. When drying is done, the clamp is removed and the stock separated into individual pads, each with a chipboard base.

6-19. The drill punch makes holes for a ring binder. It punches through several hundred sheets at a time.

Padding is done to the trimmed size, and the glue may be put on either the long or the short side, depending on the design of the pad. Pads of about one hundred sheets would be a normal thickness and are probably not too thick to be handled easily in writing. But the number of sheets varies, and the pads may be made up in any thickness consistent with the design and use.

Notebook covers or looseleaf binders are often chosen because of the convenience with which sheets can be removed or added for updating. The sheets are drilled to fit the binder spacing, and usually the cover is given special treatment for a finished look. Stickers made of adhesive sheets may be used for this purpose.

Plastic bindings are an extra that is useful for holding permanent notebooks and presentations. A common plastic binding is the spiral one, requiring a special machine to make the holes and feed in the spine.

Sometimes sheets of paper are left loose and placed in an envelope within a folder. The sheets may be of different sizes or folded and are taken out for separate handling. A press kit might be treated this way, accommodating photos for reproduction.

Binding is useful in many diverse products. In the quantities customary to instant printing examples might be scripts, studies,

6-20. Two different plastic bindings are displayed here. One has a continuous plastic spine, and the other is the familiar spiral binding.

6-21. Different styles and colors in hole-binder covers are shown here. This printer will hot-stamp headings on them in colors.

surveys, sales presentations, and press releases, to note but a few of the kinds of items with enough pages to need binding.

Staple bindings may be made in any convenient size by trimming. The largest size possible for a booklet within instant-printing formats is 8½ × 11 inches, and this would utilize a 17 × 11 inch sheet. As additional sheets are printed, they are folded and gathered inside each other and then bound with staples. Smaller sizes are more often done with folds and trimmed, because this reduces both the labor and the cost.

Padding can also be done in any convenient size. The 8½ × 11 inch size is popular for forms, as is the quarter-page size for smaller forms, though they can be sized smaller by trimming the instant printing sizes.

Ready-made covers, including ring binders and plastic bindings, are usually designed to fit the 8½ × 11 inch size, with some bindings available at the half-sheet size. Ready-made folders with flap pockets and envelopes are also predicated on the standard format of 8½ × 11 inches.

When booklets are made up from a number of signatures, or separate printed sheets, these will be gathered by hand into the proper order for binding. Here is the opportunity to use paper for its effect on the design. For instance, to use a colored cover with parchment as a title sheet and the text on bond will help make an attractive presentation. When booklets are made with folds only, there is no opportunity to use different papers. The quantities envisioned for this treatment are those that would be used for presentations. Such things as sales booklets would in all likelihood require too large a quantity for such handwork.

Binding, folding, sizing, and trimming are done on a short-term basis because of the immediacy of the printing and the quantity, but the handwork involved in the various steps does take time.

When a sheet is printed on both sides, it takes time for the ink to dry on one, before the other can be printed. Again, the binding and trimming can be done only when the second printing is dry. Depending on drying conditions, this usually involves a day for each printing. The special work of folding, gathering, binding, and trimming is done at the end of the day, when no more while-you-wait orders are taken. Printing that requires these operations takes at least three or four days to complete. This should be planned for, if there is a deadline involved, because there is no way to speed up the drying time.

Through instant printing it is now possible to produce limited-quantity, special-purpose pamphlets and booklets or to make finished presentations at a reasonable price in less time than was formerly possible.

QUALITY 7

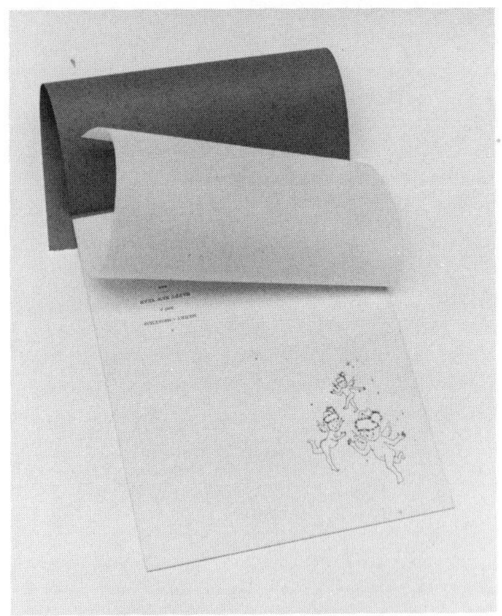

7-1. Art for instant printing should be clean and protected. The piece shown here has both a tissue for notations and a protective cover. With handling the protective cover will prove a valuable addition.

The values that provide communications excellence for instant printing art are similar to traditional graphic arts values. The pursuit of quality in the preparation of art in this process will get the best results, just as it does with traditional processes.

The reproduction process necessarily contributes to the appearance of the product, but the quality of graphic art and design can be seen separately from the reproduction process. Fine quality is essential to communication. There is a synergism that stems from the way art and communication use the process that is an art form in itself. And this adds a unique quality to the instant-printing process.

The immediacy and availability of instant printing give new importance to convenience, but this conflicts with traditional values of printing that put reproduction quality ahead of convenience. No matter how convenient, though, everyone wants effective communication, and graphic design and reproduction must be sufficiently good to achieve it. The process may put limitations on reproduction, when compared to other methods of graphic reproduction, but when well done and taken on its own terms, the process shows a unique craft quality.

The limitations of the instant printing process impel a different approach, one more like that of early letterpress printing, since the one-step provision of the film system requires the art to be complete.

At the same time, these limitations make financially feasible the production of certain kinds of items in small quantities that were not possible before.

The more knowledgeable about instant printing art the user is, the better the quality of product and the more products that can be done. This simple and dependable process places the user in control of the quality of the graphics and of the communication. The user relationship to this process shows an energy that is expected to continue to improve and increase the ways in which instant printing is used. This is borne out by the continuing expansion of instant printing centers and by the services they offer.

Printers often keep portfolios of their top work, and many instant printers have display boards of the best pieces to come through their shops. These boards show the quality of instant printing art and form an impressive display.

MISTAKES TO WATCH OUT FOR

Paste-up is the primary method of preparing instant-printing art. Even typewritten material can benefit from respacing while being pasted up. The finished paste-up is the complete, final art for the product. In the printing process it is difficult to compensate for shortfalls on the paste-up, so mistakes at that level that will blemish reproduction must be watched for with care.

It should be obvious that the paste-up must be clean in order to lead to spotless reproduction, yet this is one of the easiest errors to make. Rubber cement overlooked at the edges of pasted material may not be obvious at first, but its stickiness collects dirt that can reproduce. Through static electricity the edges of invisible mending tape will inevitably also collect enough dust to reproduce. For the sake of cleanliness, it is sometimes easier to use an adhesive that is sprayed on before the edges are trimmed. When cutting takes place after the adhesive is applied, no adhesive should appear beyond the edge, unless the paper is burnished so heavily that adhesive is squeezed out. Such heavy rubbing might also damage the image. For application before cutting, either wax adhesive and one-coat rubber cement is useful.

The alignment on the paste-up is what will appear on the product. It is necessary, therefore, to have pasted pieces accurately positioned, and a T square is the easiest way to be sure of this. If the edges are cut true to the image, it is always easier to align the paste-up. There is a tendency to align to the edge of the

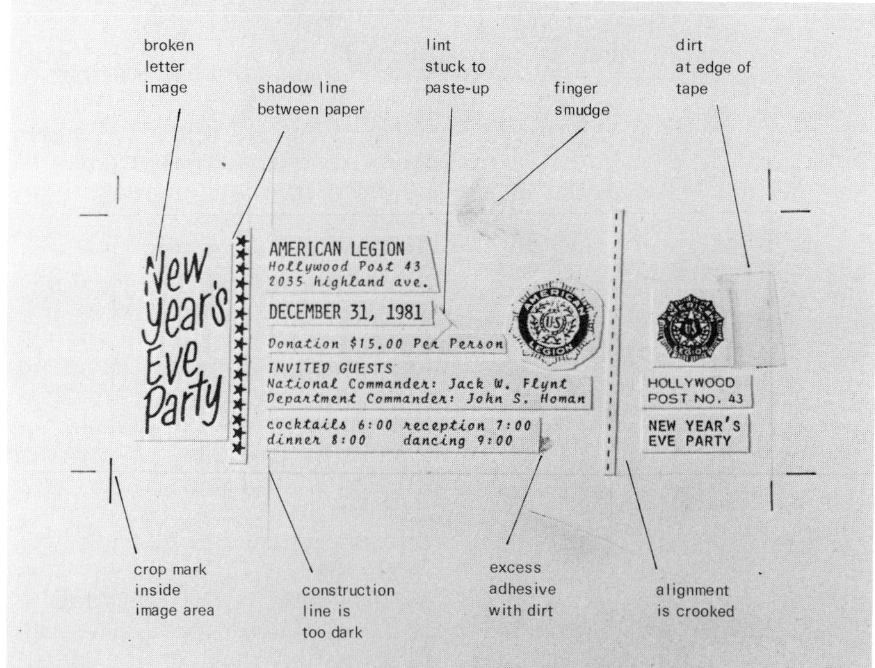

7-2. These common paste-up problems can reproduce and spoil the effect of the design. The paste-up for the ticket, though done quickly and inexpensively, was not originally executed this way. Remedies are *left to right, top to bottom*: retouch broken letter with ink; opaque shadow area with white paint; remove lint; clean up smudge with kneaded eraser or white paint; remove tape and use adhesive or double-sided tape underneath; opaque crop mark extension into image area; erase or opaque construction line; clean up excess adhesive; remove dotted line and re-paste in better alignment.

paper instead of the image on the paper, and where there is no conflict between the two, there is nothing to fool the eye.

The edges of pasted pieces of paper cast a shadow, which often shows on work done with a copier. The instant printing reproduction process gets around this with much better lighting. Lights are placed at 45 degrees along the full length of the copy, producing reflected light and eliminating shadows. Very thick pieces of paper are still a problem, and any shadow registers on the printing plate as a black line.

When two pieces of paper nearly butt against each other, the valley formed between them will create a shadow. This is most easily avoided by overlapping the edges of adjoining pieces of paper or by moving them far enough apart to avoid the shadow. When this is impossible, the valley between the pieces of paper should be filled with white paint, such as typing-correction fluid. It is also possible to sand thick pieces of paper down from the back, before the adhesive is applied. Made of wood fibers, paper sands easily.

Construction lines, made to assist in aligning the paste-up, will not reproduce when a non-reproducing blue is used. If not, these lines must be erased.

Paste-up copy that has different densities of black presents a problem in reproduction exposure. It must either average the different densities or be strong enough to capture the lightest.

Copy of uneven density can be compensated for to some extent by holding back the blackest portions with dodging, a technique that covers the strongest parts, while continuing the exposure of the weakest areas. This technique takes judgment, and for it there is an extra charge. For copy of extremely uneven density two printing plates can be made. Separate printings are then done, with each plate in register with the other to produce the complete copy. It is usually easier and less expensive to correct the paste-up, bringing the density to a more equal value.

When colors are used along with the normal black and white copy, there is always a density problem. The single exception is red, which registers as black on orthochromatic film.

Too much erasing over black ink lines removes some of the pigment, reducing its density. Of course, only the lightest erasing should be done over typewritten material, lest it smear.

Different background colors for strong black copy will make a difference because of their different light reflectance. Light blue and light yellow backgrounds are the easiest to deal with. In the worst case, yellow tape will show with deep exposure.

Halftones, or veloxes, require an accurate exposure to hold the tone values and should have only even density, black-and-white copy with them.

The plates used for the instant-printing process can be scraped to remove some blemishes or shadow lines, but not major ones. The process is designed to handle straightforward reproduction from even-density copy, and the paste-up will get the best reproduction if it adheres to this.

BEST RESULTS

The best results are obtained from the instant printing process when the paste-up is done on bright, white, matte paper with the copy image a dense black. This produces the crispest reproduction and retains with high fidelity fine, delicate originals.

Differences in paper reflectance alter the exposure, and though the instant printing film has enough latitude to accept some variations of exposure, the sensitivity is such that different reflectances will register a change in line resolution. To illustrate, when a glossy line photostat and a matte line photostat—both with the same ideal black image—are shot together, the greater light reflectance from the glossy photostat causes it to overexpose if the matte photostat is given the correct exposure. For this reason, photostats and veloxes should be on a matte paper that matches the reflectance of the bright, white, background paper.

The reproduction image of black ink should be uniformly dense and equally black. While no black image is a pure, non-reflecting black, the reproduction is produced by the difference of reflectance in the image area.

Veloxes should be used for halftone art, unless what is wanted is the special effect of line resolution, in which only the deepest shadows in the tonal art reproduce as black line. They should be no finer than 85-line screen for the best reproduction, and the lightest tones should have a definite dot that is sufficient for reproduction.

Inevitably some pieces of art present reproduction problems and should be redone before being included in the paste-up. To do them over the kind of copier known as a duplicator may provide a suitable reconciliation of tone and density at minimum cost. This particular copier is suggested because of its reproduction system. Otherwise, the problem material may be shot with a negative and a photostat made. Color copy can also be handled this way. The goal in redoing art is to see that everything used in the paste-up has an image of approximately the same density.

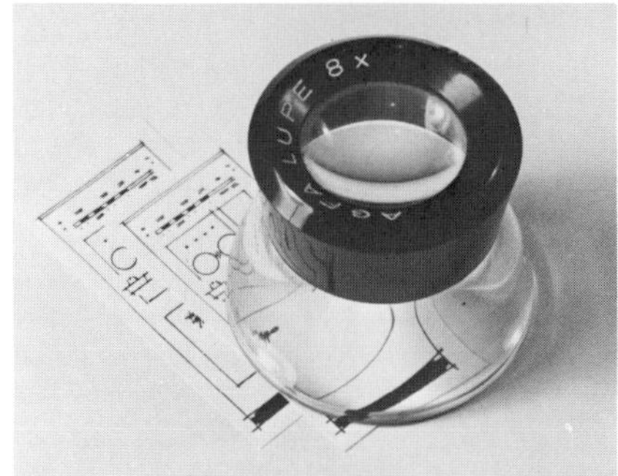

7-3. Starting with art and copy of even reflectance is important because of its effect on exposure. It takes a sharp eye or magnification to see the actual differences in the original copy.

While typewriter correcting fluid doesn't look attractive when splashed around a paste-up, it should be used when necessary to clean up the art. The fluid is used to blank out dirt, paper flecks, and construction lines in the non-reproducing areas of the paste-up.

By preparing the art efficiently an effort is made at the start to remove problems and to present even reflectance and image density. It is by eliminating difficulties at the paste-up level that the one-step process can operate most efficiently.

But this process does have its limitations. The direct reproduction process is designed for uniform copy, and the one-step simplification is not designed to cope with aberrations. The latitude of the film for the direct printing plate is wide enough to handle some variation, but it can manage only one exposure. Staying inside that latitude with uniform copy is the way to a fine end product.

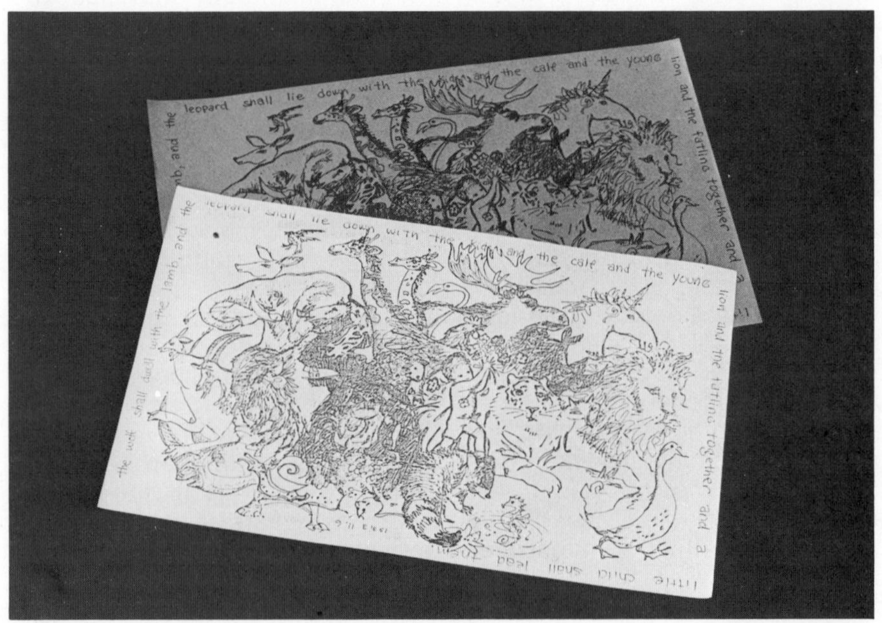

7-4. It is simpler to redo problem copy than to try to compensate for different densities in one paste-up. Here a piece of art on a deep color background is successfully copied on the copier. The resulting art is a pure black and white, and can now be incorporated in the paste-up without further difficulty. The copier can be adjusted for different densities, when each piece is taken singly.

LIMITATIONS

Because it is a direct plate process, instant printing has many limitations. The process has been designed to achieve economy through simplicity, and the one-step printing plate prevents manipulation of the printing material. The virtue of economy is at the root of the limitations ascribed to instant printing, and the system is predicated on a utilitarian quality suitable for duplication. The surprise is the quality that the process is capable of. The resolution of film for the direct-process printing-plate film is the same as ordinary high-contrast film, and under ideal conditions this is evident.

But printing is seldom done under ideal conditions, and this is where the differences of quality in the printed product become apparent. The direct process has only simple means to cope with the less-than-ideal copy that it may have to deal with. The instant printer does not control the preparation of material.

It is possible to achieve a consistently high quality with instant printing, if the art is of uniformly high quality; this of course is the way to deal with the limitations of instant printing. The paste-up should be prepared with the best reproduction quality in mind, so as to use the one-step process at its optimum. Reproduction quality should be seen as a consideration separate from the aesthetic quality of the product design.

If it is reasonable for a printer to make different negatives with different exposures to prepare a printing plate for high-quality printing, it is just as reasonable to prepare a paste-up by using photoprints of art that were prepared with different exposures, since it is at the paste-up level that control can be exercised on the printing process. One procedure is no more expensive than the other.

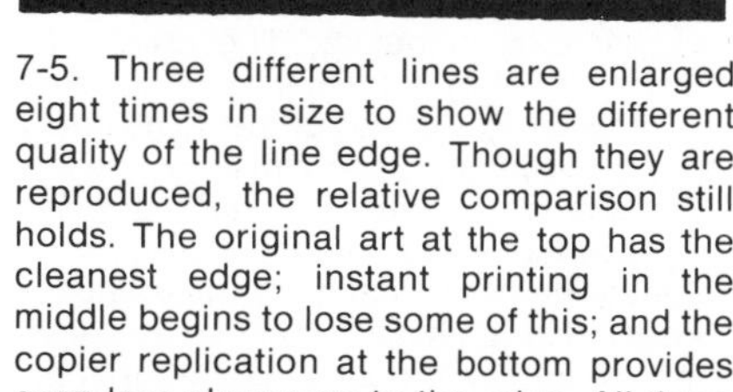

7-5. Three different lines are enlarged eight times in size to show the different quality of the line edge. Though they are reproduced, the relative comparison still holds. The original art at the top has the cleanest edge; instant printing in the middle begins to lose some of this; and the copier replication at the bottom provides even less cleanness to the edge. All three samples are a good, strong black on white, and the two duplications do much better than other copying processes.

Better copy then results in finer printing. However, because the instant-printing process is considered an economy process, this isn't done, and the price of negatives the printer uses are buried in the cost of the printing.

Each limitation imposed on instant printing by the system can be overcome by adding custom work to the process. Much of what can be done with film for black-and-white art can be duplicated in the preparation of a paste-up, but for the instant-printing system the paste-up must present the complete art.

It is the direct printing plate and the format of materials that makes printing available to the public as an over-the-counter, retail business. The difference between it and other printing is that it is the user who decides whether to spend extra money in preparing art. The user makes the decision on how far to go to obtain better quality or an extended range of applications. At some point in the extension of applications for instant printing, the process is misused. It would be better to use a printing process suited to wider application.

The primary distinction in application is in regard to quantity. The bigger the quantity, the less the preparation cost means in the unit cost of the product. It is this consideration, the quantity, that leads to the choice of economical preparation in small-quantity

7-6. This is an enlargement of the two pieces of art under the glass in 7-3. Notice the difference between the film image at the bottom and the instant printing image at the top. The printing process is not designed for the same fidelity as film.

printing and permits a finer preparation in large-quantity printing. The different application also saves costs when compared to instant printing.

The instant-printing process is adapted to small-quantity printing. It would be a mistake to change this retail approach into something else, disturbing the effectiveness of the system. At the same time there is no reason to accept quality limitations, because quality can be controlled in the preparation of the art.

It is possible for the knowledgeable user to bypass the paper inventory supplied by the printer, but it is more convenient to use suppliers adapted to this role. The convenience of the retail format, the volume purchases that keep costs low, and the speed are what make the system of production so valuable.

Some jobs shouldn't be done with instant printing, because the requirements are outside the limits of the system. It can be extended by the knowledgeable user, but some products and processes are better adapted to the commercial job printer. There is a considerable difference between instant printing and commercial job printing, even if some instant printers have moved toward the boundary between the two. The line between instant printing and job printing lies in the difference between retail and custom format, between small-quantity and large-quantity production systems, with the consequent differences in the processes used.

Small-quantity printing with the direct-plate process is not so much hemmed in by limitations as it is compelled to follow the intent of the design of the system. Complaints about the quality of work done by instant printers can be largely obviated by correct preparation of the art. The system can be extended to a variety of products, and their quality can be surprisingly good.

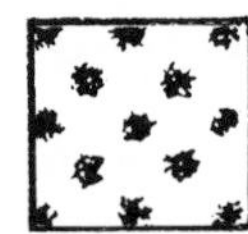

7-7. The dots in a halftone screen can vary a great deal in quality. The dots in the screen at left, greatly enlarged, are clean and regular in shape, but the same dots at the right from a printed piece are irregular with shapes broken up. Starting with a photoprint of a halftone or with dots from a printed halftone makes a difference in quality. Naturally the cleaner velox will hold its tone and reproduce better.

The line between art preparation and printing is a necessary one; the vagaries of aesthetics have always made a separation between craft and art. It is possible to see when the craft of printing is well-done, since the values are more definite than those that apply to design.

Keeping the values clear-cut, the instant printer does not enter into the preparation of art. His work is limited to the duplication of the material. If the user provides bad quality copy, the result will be bad quality printing. You can beat the system, if you control the preparation, and this is why instant printing is popular. It comes down to how you use it.

PRINTING QUALITY

Perhaps it is an oversimplification to say that instant printing will look exactly like the original copy, when any of the steps between the original and the duplicate can modify the result. Printing quality is not as automatic as pushing a button. There are many complexities in printing that have to do with the operation of the press, the ink, and the paper. The printing plate has first to be a good duplicate of the original, since no degree of printing quality can correct this deficiency. Temperature speeds up or slows down the film process, and humidity affects the printing plate and ink, which de-

7-8. Printing is not a completely mechanical process but is subject to many variables that require craft skills and judgment.

pend on moisture to work. So there is a daily need to modify the process to compensate for weather changes.

The standardization of technique and materials all help to overcome the variables of printing and tend to keep them within a manageable range. The simplification of the process helps as well, since there are fewer operations to adjust and correct. There are, however, the areas of judgment and craft. The two great sins of instant printing are overexposure of the printing plate and over-inking of the press. The inclination to do both results from an effort to get good line resolution from fuzzy or gray copy. Presenting the printer with sharp, dense, uniform copy means getting the optimum by keeping the system centered, instead of overbalancing it to compensate for deficiencies. Of the two, film exposure has more latitude than inking.

The user can judge these two aspects by the amount of ink on the print. If the inking is, as it should be, just sufficient for coverage, but the image presents a loss of fine detail with a closure and fattening of the lines, the plate was overexposed. The reverse is true, if fine line detail begins to break up and the lines are not complete. Too much ink can also block up detail on a properly exposed plate, and this looks like overexposure, except that there is too much ink on the print.

With the pre-cut paper format used for instant printing, it is necessary for the printer to align exactly the plate and paper feed, so that the image on printed version is positioned in the same way as the original. When the paste-up is on paper of exactly the same size as the format, the position is obvious. But if the paste-up is done on an oversized board, as many are, the paste-up should have the crop marks of the format's perimeter clearly indicated, so that the image can be aligned with them.

When the format size is trimmed, the trim marks should be indicated outside the paste-up at the edge. A paste-up is often done on an oversized board to allow room for marks and instructions. Do not show construction lines on the art, unless they are done in non-reproducing blue. The printer has no way to remove them and can only cover them before shooting the printing plate, making more work.

Instructions to the printer can be shown on the art in two ways. Indications, construction lines, and notes can be drawn and written at the borders of the art outside the area of the format. Or instructions can be written on a flap of tracing paper that folds over the art to protect it and back out of the way for shooting.

Since most instant-printing work is presented over the counter, instructions can be given then. Usually they are relayed on the purchase order or carried verbally. In the latter case, to write the instructions on the art is a guarantee that nothing is lost in the verbal process.

The majority of instant printers bend over backwards to satisfy their customers. With normal art there is seldom a problem. It is when there are problems with the copy that a job may be undertaken only at the customer's risk. Here too, the user has control over the process and makes the decisions.

Any printing process tends to lose some detail and to smooth out very fine irregularities of line seen at the edges of the copy, when looked at through a magnifying glass. The highest quality instant printing of excellent copy will also lose some fine detail. But it should be remembered that the process is not designed for the best reproduction of very fine detail, that it was designed to duplicate simple line copy. This it does suprisingly well.

7-9. The consequences of over-inking are seen at the right. Notice the lines in the trumpet and the fingers. Perhaps more subtle is the change in the expression of the face.

INDEX